CRUMMEY V IRELAND

CRUMMEY V IRELAND

FRANK CRUMMEY

WITH ANNE STOPPER

LONDUBH BOOKS

First published in 2009 by

Londubh Books

18 Casimir Avenue, Harold's Cross, Dublin 6w, Ireland

www.londubh.ie

1 3 5 4 2

Cover by bluett

Origination by Londubh Books

Printed in Ireland by ColourBooks, Baldoyle Industrial Estate, Dublin 13

ISBN: 978-1-907535-01-7

This book is dedicated to the two most important and influential women in my life – my mother, Elizabeth, and my wife, Evelyn – and to my family.

When I was a child, my mother instilled in me a value system that has stood to me throughout my life. She taught me that, while I might not be better than anybody, equally, nobody was better than me. She told me that you didn't need money for happiness and that if you ever saw something that was wrong, you should do everything in your power to correct it. I have tried to live by this philosophy and I like to think that she would be proud of the life I've led to date.

I also want to dedicate the book to my wife, Evelyn, who married me in 1961, against the wishes of her family and many others. In the almost fifty years we've been married, she has loved me and supported me through the highs and lows of the many campaigns I've fought. Her sense of humour, her strength and her determination have helped to ensure that our value system has been passed on to our five children and ten grandchildren.

I wish to thank my children, Elizabeth, Deirdre, Edel, Jane and Frank, for listening to me recounting the stories of my life over and over again as they grew up. I would, however, like to tell them that just because I finally listened to what they said and wrote the book, it doesn't mean I won't continue to regale them with these same stories for years to come.

ACKNOWLEDGEMENTS

I wish to ackowledge the many people who assisted me in preparing this book, especially the following:

Anne Stopper, my friend, for her encouragement and enthusism. Without her I would not have had the words to write this book.

Sean Burke, a neighbour on Kilfenora Road, who reminded me of the words of the song, 'The Scabies Are all over Dublin'.

Margaret Ahern, of the Irish Institute of Legal Executives, who suggested the title of this book, *Crummy v Ireland*.

Mick Brophy, my son-in-law, for his chauffeuring, typing, proofreading and unofficial editorial advice.

Pat Byrne, my friend of more than thirty years, for reading the first draft of this book and being very objective and fair in her criticisms.

The Irish Institute of Legal Executives for its assistance in launching this book.

CONTENTS

FOREWORD BY FR BRIAN D'ARCY C.P.

Towards the end of Frank Crummey's enthralling memoir he sums up a life spent bringing hope to the hopeless by admitting that reading the recent Ryan and Murphy Reports left him with just a twinge of guilt. 'For me, the conclusions of both reports have demonstrated what I'd always known was as much a tragedy as the abuse itself: a whole nation's ability to stand silently by and let it happen,' he writes. Many of us are tortured by the same kind of guilt – and so we should be. Personally I need to confess, 'What I've done,' and even more significantly, 'What I failed to do.'

I don't know of a single citizen in Ireland who did more to help the abused, the downtrodden, the voiceless and the people who got a bad deal than Frank Crummey. He was one of the first people to name the guilty – the arrogant Catholic clergy scandalously abusing power and status and the spineless politicians who forfeited power to them.

In *Crummey v Ireland* Frank relates a selection of the many thousands of cases he has been involved in. This is no self-trumpeting arrogant book. It is the true story of the man I know Frank Crummey to be.

Frank was born and raised in Kilfenora Road in Kimmage. For twelve years it was part of my area ßwhen I was a priest starting out in the newly-formed parish of Mount Argus. Frank mentions that he knew every one of the hundred and two families on Kilfenora Road. So did I. For part of my tenure, the Crummey family lived in one of these houses. The neighbours, whom he speaks so highly of here, were known to me. I learned so much from all of them as I visited them on a daily basis.

I am not sure if Frank will want me to tell this story but I'll tell it anyway. Frank always had difficulty with the Church's abuse of power but he set aside all his problems in the interest of compassion. He could always be relied upon to do the right thing, as could Evelyn and all their children. When we organised open-air Masses at the corner of Kilfenora and Clonfert Roads, right up to the end of the 1980s, one of the main helpers was Frank Crummey. He supported every genuine effort to make people's lives more meaningful. I've always had the greatest personal admiration for Frank Crummey. You don't have to agree with everything a man does or says in order to recognise his courage and his authenticity. Frank is the real deal and always was.

His book is a wonderful if often disturbing read. It tells the story of an Ireland that is simply not recognisable to young people now. But if you want to find out how it could happen that the abuses outlined in the Ryan Report and the Murphy Report were allowed to happen in Dublin, read Frank's book and you'll discover in a practical, jovial way just how hard it was to break down the superpowers of Church and state. As Frank freely admits, there were many good priests and many good politicians in the Dail. But there was a culture of arrogance that always dumped on the most vulnerable. Frank Crummey recognised this at an early age and then spent his life challenging it.

Anyone who knows Frank recognises his ability to tell a story. He reminds me of that enlightening insight of the wonderful theologian of story, John Shea, who said, 'All stories are true – some of them actually happened.' I'm sure others reading Frank's book will remember stories and incidents differently but this shouldn't diminish the truth of Frank's stories.

Frank's stories are all about people. He delights in portraying himself as the small man, literally and metaphorically. He relishes David's victories over Goliath. There is humour and there is great sadness. There is humanity and there is palpable evil. The reader is entertained and challenged. This is precisely the kind of story and the kind of book we need in Ireland today. This isn't a legal report: it's a human story of an individual who sacrificed his life and his family in the cause of justice.

Most chapters in some way come back to Frank's wonderful mother, who gave him a self-belief and confidence that he used to change the face of a very bleak society. He has been 'all things to all men'. This man, now in his seventies, takes us through a life which includes being an altar boy in Crumlin, a member of the Confraternity in Mount Argus, a loyal member of the Legion of Mary in the same church and a contented atheist now. It details a myriad occupations, which included being an army gunner, a taxi driver, a London bus driver, a lonely emigrant in Australia, an ice-cream man, a salesman for women's underwear, a postman, a social worker, a cleaner of sewers, a helper in a women's refuge and a founder-member of the Institute of Legal Executives.

Most people remember Frank in his early days on *The Late Late Show* in the mid 1960s. He was the first man to talk publicly about the cruelty of legalised corporal punishment, especially as practised by the Irish Christian Brothers. He confronted the status quo as a member of the Language Freedom Movement, which, as he says on page 79 of this book, '...was the first movement to question what was really behind the issues of how Ireland expressed itself.' Frank once famously brought *The Late Late Show* to a close by shouting into a camera, 'As I sit here tonight, the Irish Christian Brothers are abusing our children.' And that was in 1967.

Many of us should feel guilty that we didn't shout stop. But Frank Crummey *did* shout stop and many of us were convinced he was exaggerating. He challenged the views of the Catholic Church in a healthy way and I know his arguments helped me to rethink the accepted morality of sexuality. Frank saw the beauty of sex as a wonderful gift from God, where many others saw only sin.

Frank says he is an atheist now and he is at peace because of his conviction. Today, believers and non-believers have learned how to work together, live together and most of all how to respect honestly-held differences.

There are many crucial chapters but for me the one that showed that Frank's story was moving in a new direction was the chapter on Reform. It's the one that puts the spotlight on the dark and sinister era many of us took for granted.

I am privileged that Frank asked me to write this foreword for his book. It's a thrilling read which will make you angry, especially, if like me, you have lived through the times he describes so well. His book is uplifting, pointed, human and delightfully hopeful. It's a rare privilege to meet a man who has done so much good and for whom compassion was not just a word but a way of life.

Thank you, Frank, and thank you, Evelyn. May your love go on for ever!

Brian D'Arcy C.P.
January 2010

INTRODUCTION

The dogs didn't go around in pairs on Kilfenora Road, like the locals said they did on some of the other, rougher roads in Kimmage, when Frank Crummey grew up there in the 1940s and 1950s. In fact, Kilfenora was a particular road in a particular area where many people who were coming up in the world were moving from the tenements into the newly-built corporation estates and living in a house for the first time. But for Frank's mother, Elizabeth, things were different. For Elizabeth, moving to Kilfenora was a step down.

Elizabeth Crummey's situation in the 1930s was without name or description even though its existence was obvious, like a hazy blur in an overexposed photograph. She collected old, discarded rubber from bicycle tires and mended her children's shoes on her cobbler's last. She fixed trousers for Frank that ended up with more patch than original fabric in the seat. She ran her own business from the house and performed all the same daily tasks, small and large, mundane and heroic, as mothers the world over. Frank and his three sisters never even realised it was unusual that their father wasn't there.

It wasn't so much that Elizabeth Crummey was struggling to make the best of a bad situation as that she didn't seem to see the situation as all that bad in the first place. Where others saw and sometimes pitied a deserted wife, she enjoyed her independence as queen of her castle – she didn't have to answer to anyone in her own house, like so many other women did back then. While others whispered about the misfortune of her having to move from Fairview to Kimmage, she was busy socialising with her new Kilfenora neighbours and it wasn't long before it became obvious that she belonged there as surely as if she'd been born on the street. And when others were tongue-clucking over the state of her poor fatherless children, she was telling them how great they were, persuading them that they were all little Einsteins and making sure they got the best education they possibly could.

There were no puffy red eyes, no stifled sobs behind closed doors for Frank's mother, no plastering of false, forced smiles on her face for the children's sake. Believe it or not – and some found it harder to believe than others – Elizabeth Crummey was a genuinely happy woman. Her happiness was transferred like a manufacturer's stamp of approval on to the characters of her children. Today, what Frank's mother did might be viewed as putting the best possible spin on the family's circumstances but that wouldn't be an entirely accurate description of her perception of herself and her children. Her attitude was more honest than that, reflecting what she saw as their reality with only a few alterations: tightening seams of information here or turning material over there to conceal unsightly stitches of the past. The Crummey children knew they were poor and they obviously knew they had no father in the house – but so what? Everyone on Kilfenora was poor and their father's absence was never presented as a tragedy.

As Frank meanders further into his seventies now, he sees himself in the image that his mother cultivated and maybe even created altogether: he's clever, capable, kind, healthily irreverent of authority and in possession of an even healthier ego, the result of a fabulous confidence. His stories about his mother and Kilfenora don't always make chronological sense: he starts talking about one thing of a certain time and place, then suddenly shifts settings radically, reminded by his own details about something else he must tell. The links between his stories are looser and less obvious than chronology alone. This book reflects, to an extent, his style of storytelling. It also reveals the truth that a man can become the person someone else sees him as merely *because* she sees him that way – the transformative power of a perception rooted in unconditional love.

Frank's own view of his mother is just as powerful and constant as hers was of him. Today, he finds it difficult to look at photos of her. He's a small, tough man who learned to live by his wits and who, in his youth, was just as quick to throw a punch as look at someone. But when he talks about his mother now, he pulls a handkerchief out of his pocket and turns away, running it messily and unashamedly over his face. 'Isn't it funny that of all the things in my life, the one thing I never got over was my mother,' he says but it isn't funny at all. Listening to his stories, it makes perfect sense.

Anne Stopper, January 2010

1

KILFENORA

There were a hundred and two houses on Kilfenora Road in Kimmage when I grew up there and today, at the age of seventy-three, I can tell you my old neighbours' addresses, family names and hundreds of outrageous stories about them. As I count down through the house numbers in my mind, zig-zagging back and forth across the street, I can see the doors opening and closing and the faces of the people emerging from each one. I've always had a good memory but I know its limits. I wouldn't be able to tell you the name of every child who grew up on Kilfenora Road. Between the hundred and two two-bedroom houses, there were between eight and nine hundred children.

I've been told that my stories open up each house as if it were a doll's house, with one side on hinges so that whoever is listening gets a vivid picture of the inner workings. Our next-door neighbours were the Davises and Jimmy, one of the eldest of the fourteen Davis children, played the violin late into the night every night. He'd always finish with the national anthem and then shout at the top of his voice, 'Goodnight, Crummeys!' so we'd know he was done. Jimmy had a lot of responsibility and when Mr and Mrs Davis would go on a Sunday outing – the only time during the week they had to themselves – Jimmy was in charge of the soup. One Sunday one of the youngest Davis boys came in from the garden and, for reasons known only to his young mind, decided the pot of soup was a good place for his muddy boots. Jimmy, being resourceful and used to having to find solutions for calamities, removed the boots, gave the young one a clatter and served up the soup. There was no question of wasting on Kilfenora; it just wasn't done. The little treats were simple and rare enough, so when the Davis children told me about their pot of jam, I asked to see it. It fell against the side of the bath and smashed. Disaster. There was a mad scatter to scoop it up in saucers to save it.

I loved Mrs Davis. I'd chance joining the family soup queue and when I'd get to the front she'd say, 'You're not one of mine but you can have some anyway.' Even when I broke the pendulum of the Davises' beautiful clock, the family's one shining valuable possession – I was playing with it when it came off in my hand and I panicked, shoving it back up inside and jamming the works – all Mrs Davis said to my mother was, 'Your Frankie was in my house again and he broke the clock. I'll kill him! Keep him out of my way for a day or two!'

Mr and Mrs Davis had a great romance, although they were poor like everyone else on Kilfenora and had enough children for their own football team, plus several to fill in for the injured. The Davis house was a great one for parties and Mr Davis would always sing: 'The first forty years are the hardest and then you get used to it all. There were their kids and our kids and my kids and your kids...the more we are together, the merrier we will be.'

The Davises' romance was one based on love, poverty and religion, and when the couple's declining health forced them to leave Kilfenora to move in with one of their children in their sixty-eighth year of marriage, Mr Davis still sang to his wife. Three of the Davis girls became nuns, the eldest girl a Jehovah's Witness and another of the boys a Jesuit priest. I reckon that if you had thirteen brothers and sisters you'd be tempted to join a convent, too, if only to get a bed to yourself for the first time in your life.

I remember the 'glimmer man' coming around during the war when gas was rationed and passing his hand over the top of the hob, a magician's stage gesture, to see if there was any heat on it. But the Davises didn't even have a cooker. They prepared all their meals over their small open fire because the expense of the gas was too much for them.

Small brick walls separated the houses from one another on Kilfenora and if I sat up on the one between our house and the Davises', I could look in their back window or yell, 'Ooooooo!' through the pipe that was used for overflow from their bath. 'Get off the wall, Frankie Crummey!' came the Davis reply in a bellow. There was never any overflow through their pipe because there were very seldom any baths. With the complicated system of heating pipes in the houses, it was difficult to get the water hot enough for a warm bath in the summertime and impossible in the winter.

A much bigger wall separated nearby Tonguefield Road and Blarney Park Road, just a few streets over from Kilfenora. The wall was solid concrete casing, stood about eight feet high and was there solely to divide the corporation houses from the private houses. Pure snobbery. The presence of the wall meant that if neighbours from Kilfenora or the adjacent Clonfert Road or Bangor Road wanted to get to the shops on Sundrive Road, on the other side of Blarney Park Road, they had to take a detour that was probably twice as long as if they had been able to pass through the streets the wall separated. People gradually began breaking holes in the wall large enough to push prams through but they were always patched up until the wall finally came down in the 1940s.

There was fabulous generosity between the neighbours on Kilfenora. The house that was having visitors was always obvious because it was the best furnished. Before the visitors arrived the family would make the rounds to the neighbours, knocking on doors for a loan of armchairs and tables, rearranging their sitting room as if setting the scene for a play. The granny who was visiting would be pleased that her daughter was doing well for herself but if she had ever missed the bus and had to come back to the house unexpectedly, she wouldn't have recognised the place without all the borrowed furniture. My mother had a radio, which was posh in those days on Kilfenora, and I ran a wire connected to a loudspeaker from our house to our neighbours' house at the back, the Farrells', so they could listen to the programmes too. Mrs Davis, a great friend of my mother, came over to our house every night to listen to the radio.

It wasn't until my teenage years that we got a phone but like everything else on Kilfenora, when the neighbours heard we had it, they knew they could use it to ring to make funeral arrangements or in other special circumstances. In the days before there were any phones on Kilfenora, the neighbours knew there was a house on nearby Tonguefield Road where the family would take incoming calls and then send out a messenger child to deliver them, for a fee. One neighbour lived out her affair on our phone, which was in the living room. The woman was unfazed that we could hear everything and anyway, she never expected the luxury of privacy.

On Kilfenora, everyone knew everyone else's business. We had real street theatre, every day. The scenes played themselves out through the frames of the front windows or, better still, right in the front garden. Passions, fights and name-calling – an overflow of life's episodes that the producers of today's reality television shows could only dream of matching in intensity or, more importantly, authenticity – spilled out of many doors and into the street and the audience was always riveted.

The neighbours were fantastic and I loved growing up there but Kilfenora wasn't all violins, generosity and hidden, uncultivated talents, although there was an abundance of all these. There was also the house where a wife literally jumped out her own bedroom window to avoid her husband's abusive rampage. There was the vicious woman who would attack her children with sticks and pokers. There was the house that threw a wedding party consisting of nothing but brawn sandwiches, boiled potatoes and Guinness and the mother was so drunk at the end of the night that she insisted on leaving with the married couple to go on their honeymoon to Bray. Meanwhile, the father threw stones at one of his elder sons, who was perched precariously on the roof.

There was also the infamous scabies epidemic that infested almost every house on Kilfenora and much of the surrounding area. I can't remember exactly how old I was when it happened but I think I was about ten, which would have made it the late 1940s. The local health authority decided on the treatment scheme. As more and more people became infected, a song started going around the area:

> *As I was going to work one Monday morning,*
> *I saw a woman walking very slow.*
> *I asked her could she walk a little quicker,*
> *And she said she had the scabies on her toe.*
>
> *The scabies are all over Dublin.*
> *Everywhere you look you have to scratch.*
> *Go up to Doctor Conlon in the morning.*
> *And get a ticket for the sulphur baths.*

The 'sulphur baths' was the fumigation process that the infected underwent at the Iveagh Showers near Christchurch Cathedral. Children were lined up and told to take their clothes off, while health workers coated them with a stinging sulphur solution from head to toe using big brushes. You were standing next to someone, naked, as they were painting up your goolies… with a brush. Then you put on your clothes and went home. When you were a child, there was no thought of your dignity.

One indication of the vice-grip that desperation and poverty had on some families was the centrality of the pawn shop to Kilfenora. Monday was pawn day for the Kilfenora women and they would be seen going down with their bags to the shop, Kilbride's, which was a bus ride away on Clanbrassil Street. One man who had been injured in the war pawned his prosthetic arm. Mrs Murphy, who lived across the road from our house, practically lived in the pawn but one Monday she found herself with nothing left to bring. She went to her friend Mrs Fagan, who never went to the pawn herself and Mrs Fagan lent her her husband's best suit in the hopes that he wouldn't be needing it for weeks and weeks. Sure enough her husband, a civil servant, went looking for it that same week and she was caught out.

There were all kinds of Kilfenora women: beautiful, mean, resourceful, eccentric, abused, witty, broken, kind. Sometimes the nastier ones were the most interesting. They certainly could be counted on to provide the best dramatic entertainment on the street. There was a small woman on the opposite end of Kilfenora from where we lived who regularly took her husband, who was twice her size, out to the front garden to beat him. She was known as 'the boxer.'

There was also Mrs (big) Murphy, as opposed to Mrs (little) Murphy, who was lovely but never spoke to her husband. He had done something to her and they decided to remain living together but they never spoke another word, and I mean not another word, to the day he was buried. When Mr Murphy was dying, my mother and Mrs Davis were helping to look after him and they tried to get Mrs Murphy to make peace before it was too late but she wouldn't relent.

Other women, like Mrs O'Leary, were always jovial and bore their husbands' oddities with calm patience. One day Mr O'Leary asked his wife to knit him a crew-neck jumper with extremely long arms. In those days if your husband said he wanted a jumper, you did it. Especially this husband. Mrs O'Leary finished the jumper, ironed it and folded it. That night she watched as Mr O'Leary got his new jumper, put one leg in one arm, the other through the other arm and tied it around his waist to leave his bits swinging free before getting into bed.

Another neighbour dealt with her alcoholic husband with similar patience but she was much more meek and genteel than Mrs O'Leary. Her husband was a very talented cabinet maker who had one brown eye and one blue one. He usually sang as he made his way up the street after a night in the pub but when he got home, he was known to wreak havoc.

The toughest of all the Kilfenora women and the one you would never cross if you had any sense was Mrs Sullivan. Mrs Sullivan was a very small but powerfully built woman, like a tiny vicious animal with a fabulous natural defence mechanism. The neighbours all knew that even though she was small, if she hit you a dig, you were dead. The Sullivans were a massive family and they were rough. I loved them. Mrs Sullivan had a spotlessly clean house and the most immaculate garden on the street because all the kids on Kilfenora knew she would break their legs if they were caught messing around in it. When each of the Sullivan children turned fifteen, Mrs Sullivan gave them a suitcase and threw them out. She said, 'I'll have no eejits in this house,' and packed them all off to earn their own living in England.

The Sullivans had two horses and they sold coal, logs and other essentials using the horses and their cart. It was Mr Sullivan's responsibility, under threat from Mrs Sullivan, to drive the horses. When Mr Sullivan brought the horses back at the end of the day, Mrs Sullivan would feed them before bringing them back to their stable. One day she was letting the horse named Bob drink from the basin when something startled him and he jerked his head around, spilling the water. Mrs Sullivan grabbed the basin and battered poor old Bob around the head with it, shouting, 'Yeh fuckin' cow, yeh!'

In manner Mr Sullivan was the opposite to his domineering wife but he was also totally mad. Some of the other Kilfenora kids and I liked to go on the cart with him and maybe get a log or two for our mothers at the end of the day if Mrs Sullivan wasn't looking. One day just as Mr Sullivan was finishing up, the horse's tail went up. Everybody knows when a horse's tail goes up, he's going to do something. But Mr Sullivan whipped off his cap and held it over the horse's arse. And the horse went, 'Pshweeeeeeewwwwww' – a rasper of a fart. And Mr Sullivan puts the cap straight back on his head and says, 'Excuse him.' Well, we were on the ground with laughter.

Sugar-coating any information was a completely foreign idea on Kilfenora. If you were a bad bastard, you were told you were a bad bastard, end of story. There was one funeral for a woman who had died in childbirth – not an uncommon cause of death among Kilfenora women – whose husband had been a lout. I was very young at the time and my mother brought me by the hand to the graveyard. Everyone always went to the funerals because it was a day out. The coffin was lowered into the grave and the husband was given a handful of soil to throw on to it but instead, he opted for the dramatic. 'Come back to me, Mary! Come back to me!' he shouted, as he jumped in on top of the coffin. To which someone in the group responded, 'Fill it fuckin' in! He was useless!' The row started right there in the graveyard before anyone even had time to get to the pub.

Considering the closeness of the neighbours and the fact that no topic of discussion was off-limits, it was only natural that the first person who alerted me to the fact that I was unusual because I didn't have a father was a neighbour, albeit a less well-meaning one than most. I remember her as the typical neighbour from hell who fought with every other woman on the street and was known as 'Swanny' because of her unusually long, scrawny neck. What she actually said to me was something along the lines of, 'Isn't it a terrible pity you never had a father.' It was malice that didn't quite succeed in masquerading as neighbourly sympathy. When I mentioned it to my mother, she said, 'Don't mind her. You don't need a father. You're doing fine.' And I *was* doing fine. It never entered my mind that I should have had a father because I was having such a great time with my mother and three sisters, one of them my twin, Sadie, who was born just after midnight on the day following my own birth.

My father, also Frank Crummey, was born in Belfast and joined the British army when I was three years old, shortly after my family's move to Kilfenora. He went off to war and returned to Ireland and his family for about two months when I was eight or nine. Up until then, the only stories I had heard from my mother about my father were great ones. She had convinced me and my sisters not only that our father was a hero but that he had been a lone hero fighting the Second World War with some trivial assistance from General Montgomery.

My father wasn't back with the family long before I started to see my mother's stories for what they were: fairy tales. My memories of the short time when my father was living with us aren't good ones. One night he came in from the pub drunk and I found him balancing unsteadily on a stepladder, trying to change a light bulb. One of my uncles had taught me how to change plugs and fittings and I seemed to have a knack for electrical work and small repair jobs. I was also used to being the one in the house to look after these things, so I wordlessly took the bulb from my father and finished changing it. He looked at me and said, 'Aren't you a great young lad, knowing how to do that', but I knew by his tone and the look on his face that it wasn't a compliment. Apart from Swanny, I hadn't encountered many people on Kilfenora whose facial expressions fought against the words coming out of their mouths, so when it happened, I noticed.

When my father emigrated to England, leaving the family and the country for good, I was relieved to be getting on with our lovely, happy lives on Kilfenora with my mother, sisters and, of course, the neighbours.

The other thing my mother convinced me of when I was young was my own genius. Her completely unconditional and unwavering affection built up solid sand-bag barriers of confidence in me that, I see now, protected me from the brutality of some of the Christian Brothers in my primary school, Crumlin CBS, and also those in my secondary school in Synge Street. I found myself often enough at the back of the class during one particular year in primary school. Although I didn't realise it as a child, I'm dyslexic. The Brother teaching me that year didn't have much patience with slow readers, so two other boys at the back of the class and I were constantly told we were stupid. The difference was that the other boys believed the Christian Brother while I would look at him and think, 'What an idiot. Doesn't he know I'm a genius?' My mother had told me as much and there was no way I was going to believe the Christian Brother over my own mother.

At CBS, there was brutality in the forms of sexual, physical and mental abuse but I managed to avoid anything that was severely damaging. For reasons unknown, I had an instinct for identifying which Brothers to avoid, men who were later caught sexually abusing boys. Dogs could smell fear; I could smell phoney. I found I was also quite good at taking a grain of truth and fashioning it into a nice excuse, plump with plausibility. One Brother who I knew was not to be trusted asked me to stay after school one afternoon to help him put up posters. I replied, 'I have no father. I have to go home and help my mother.' Whether I did or not, how could the Brother say no?

Brothers who were actually caught in the act of abusing boys were never barred from teaching but transferred to other schools in the area and everything was hushed up, swept under the rug and deliberately ignored. Since I became an adult, one of my favourite philosophers is Edmund Burke, who said, 'All that is necessary for the triumph of evil is that good men do nothing.' Today, I can see that the abusive Christian Brothers needed help but the rest of them deserved jail. Covering up such horrendous abuse both condoned and perpetuated it, spreading the responsibility for it throughout the entire order and making too many of the 'good men' of Burke's imagination into cowards – and villains too.

I received my fair share of beatings in Synge Street CBS, my secondary school. Occasionally the Brothers there would take the class to Archbishop Byrne's Hall across the street to see a film and one of the films we went to was a biography of the boxer Joe Palooka. Shortly after the film began, my teacher stood up and said, 'Everyone in my class, we're leaving now,' with no further explanation. I stayed where I was – I had paid the admission fee and I wanted to see how it turned out. The next day my teacher had another Brother hold me while he battered me. Usually the boys in my class would either bend over or hold out their hands in submission to beatings by the Brothers but I could never do it. My mother had done a good job convincing me of my greatness and had instilled in me the intrinsic sense of dignity that such a label carries. So I was hit all the harder for insolence. It turned out that my teacher had objected to the scenes where a young girl in tights and a two-piece skirt-and-top outfit walked around the boxing ring holding placards with the round numbers. I, and probably most of the rest of the boys in the class, hadn't even noticed the girl. I would have been the first to admit it if I had but at that age I was more interested in the fighting scenes.

There were a few other boys in the class who resisted the Brothers' authority. There was one Brother in Synge Street who was particularly hypocritical. One day he was demonstrating to the class the correct position we should sleep in, with our arms crossed over our chests and said that to sleep any differently was a mortal sin. I felt a tap on my shoulder from the boy who sat behind me, a butcher's son, to tell me he'd dropped his pencil.

When I bent to pick it up for him, I saw that the boy had his penis in one hand underneath the desk. He whispered to me, '*That's* the way you sleep.' I'm awestruck, even today, at his combination of courage and foolhardiness. If he'd have been caught, he wouldn't have been beaten. He was dead. Expelled, expelled, expelled, dead, dead, dead. In those days, if you looked sideways, you got battered.

Although CBS could be brutal, there were some decent Brothers there who told good stories and would strike a boy only if provoked rather than for the enjoyment of it or out of simple habit like some of the other Brothers. But Synge Street was another story. On Kilfenora and in many working-class Dublin neighbourhoods then, it was rare for children to go to school a day past their fourteenth birthdays. My family was different because my mother had always wanted her children to go to secondary school, so when I got into Synge Street secondary at the age of twelve, two years earlier than most students left primary school, she was thrilled. I may have been thrown to the back of the class often but enough of the Brothers realised I was smart enough to handle the work. Unfortunately, I hated every minute at Synge Street. The Brothers there were particularly vicious and consistently cruel. There was one Brother who insisted on emphasising the fact that I was from Kimmage – and what could anyone expect from Kimmage?

It wasn't long after starting at Synge Street that I decided there were lots of better things to do with my time, none of which involved a schoolroom. Since I could do no wrong in my mother's eyes, she hadn't the tiniest suspicion that I wasn't at school. I could have set fire to the house and she would have said I needed to warm myself up. I designed my days to include a range of reflective, physical and cultural activities. If it took my fancy to watch the boats go in and out at the docklands, as it often did, I'd come home covered in coal dust. I'd walk into the house and my mother would say to one of the neighbours who might be visiting, 'My goodness, doesn't he get very dirty on his way home from school.' And the neighbours would be rocking with laughter, knowing I hadn't seen a school in weeks.

I also liked museums. I had an arrangement with a porter at the National Museum that when I arrived at the museum he'd put my schoolbag in a press for me. And I'd tour the museums for the day rather than go to school. Occasionally, when I felt like exercise, I went out to Herbert Park to play football with a like-minded student who went to a neighbouring school. One day we hid our schoolbags in a derelict house on Harcourt Road and went off to the park, returning later that afternoon to find the house demolished. My friend was worried but I knew I could tell my mother my bag had fallen off the back of my bike and she'd believe me, because in her eyes whatever I said to her was true. The school sent letters home about my absences but I intercepted them and had another arrangement with a friend of mine who could write very well that he would do the replies. I had every disease known to man and undoubtedly some that weren't but I remember making guest appearances at school every now and then. I showed up to science class once, on an exam day, quite by chance. The teacher wrote the questions on the board and I knew the answers to the first two. I jotted them down on my paper, jumped up and, while the teacher still had his back to the class, displayed it and said, 'Answers, one and two, right, I'm off!' leaving cartoonish punctuation marks in the air, road-runner style and a few loose papers floating behind me for emphasis.

The best thing that happened to me was that I was invited to leave Synge Street. They said I was a bad influence.

Elizabeth Mangan, like my father, was a Belfast native and she had met him while he was a political prisoner in Crumlin Road prison – some friend or another had suggested she go up to visit him, unwittingly bringing about the meeting on which the rest of her life hinged. My grandfather, also Frank Crummey, a schoolteacher, was heavily involved in IRA activities in Belfast during the first two decades of the 1900s and for a time he was in charge of intelligence operations. My father followed in his own father's footsteps and found himself in trouble at a young age, charged with the murder of Freddie Fox and attempted murder as a result of his increasing activities as an IRA man. He was on remand in Crumlin Road but received an amnesty as a result of the Treaty of 1922 and thought it prudent to get out of town. I can see the contradiction between my father's involvement with the IRA when he was a young man and his decision to join the British Army during the Second World War but I think it's one of those things for which there probably isn't a simple explanation. I never had much of a chance to discuss such things – or anything, really – in much depth with my father.

In a move that proved he was not a man who cared much for convention or doing the expected thing, my father joined the Garda Síochána as a recruiting sergeant after his release from prison and moved with his new wife to Louisburg in County Mayo. Even in the early days of their marriage, his drinking problem was serious enough. My parents moved to a house in Fairview in north Dublin but it was only a year or two until they were evicted; my father had drunk too much of the rent money. The move to Kilfenora came after this eviction and shortly after that he went off to war. He was so unlikely a candidate for the British Army that his joining, although I know it was intentional on his part, almost seems an accident.

My parents' wedding reception had been in the posh Shelbourne Hotel and the family still has the receipt that reads, 'One room with electric light.' By my mother's account, it was a fine, idyllic, sepia-toned-postcard of a romance. My father played the violin, bagpipes and piano and was a good singer. He would get a boat and take my mother down the Lagan, singing songs like 'My Lagan Love' to her. Even though my mother loved my father till the day she died, those days were the best of their time together. His alcoholism and his experiences in the war were stacked against the chances that he'd be able to come back to Ireland and live happily ever after with his family. As a young twenty-something in London, I met him briefly after not seeing him for more than a decade. He remains a man about whom I know very little and understand even less.

Although the term 'single mother' didn't even exist during my childhood, that's what my mother undeniably was. She supported her four children with a little business that she set up doing 'club dockets' for the neighbours. In a sense, it was the cottage industry precursor to the credit card. If a neighbour wanted something from a nearby shop but didn't have the money to hand, my mother would write them a docket for the amount of money and the shop in turn would give her a small commission on the docket. The neighbours would then pay her directly every week until the debt was cleared. Most people who did club dockets in those days would also charge the neighbours a commission and there was a lot of ripping-off going on but my mother never overcharged the neighbours and was still able to support the family on her income.

That's not to say she didn't struggle. She'd do her weekly shopping at Corcoran's, a grocery shop on Sundrive Road that later changed hands and became Twomey's. Every week she bought the essentials – butter, tea, sugar and bread. The manager of the shop back then was Helena Twomey, a Cork woman. Ms Twomey noticed as time went on that my mother was buying less and less every week. One day when she was shopping, Ms. Twomey asked her to come to the end of the shop to meet Mr Corcoran, the owner.

When Mr Corcoran asked why she was buying less than she used to, my mother explained that it was due to the fact that she didn't have as much money as she used to.

'You buy what you always bought,' he said. 'And if you never pay us back, it doesn't matter.'

My mother occasionally did buy more than she had the money to pay for but she kept a little black book keeping account of all that she owed and, being a Belfast woman, she eventually paid back every penny. On Saturday nights during the summer, Miss Twomey used to close the shop, get on her bicycle and come up to our house to sit in the front window with my mother, wondering if there would be any fights on the road that night. She'd often bring a small pot of jam, a huge luxury during the war years when there wasn't a shilling to be had and even many of the basics, like eggs, were hard to come by.

So my mother was never completely alone because of her kindness and good humour. People just wanted to be around her. Her status as a single parent seemed to afford the family some special treatment from the neighbours. Mr Farrell, the neighbour to whose house I had rigged up the radio wire, soldered makeshift handles on to tin cans for us during the war when there were no real cups to be had. He knew that we had no man in the house to look after such little things and little things meant so much more during the war when they were all anyone had. The young boys on the road used to fancy a game of stealing all the front gates, which were easily uprooted, and throwing them in a spiky pile at the end of the street for the neighbours to sift through and reclaim later. Our gate remained untouched. There was a code of honour among the boys that whispered like a conscience in their young, pink ears, 'It's unfair to play tricks on the houses where there's no man to sort things out.' It didn't hurt that my mother let the boys use her back garden as an escape route if they were caught playing football in the street on Sundays, which was technically illegal, and the Gardaí chased them through the neighbourhood.

My mother was very close to my father's family, several members of which also lived in Dublin, including my granny. My mother visited them every Thursday afternoon and was closer to them than her own family. Following a tradition of the time, she, the eldest of her family, had been reared by her grandmother instead of her parents, away from her own sisters. After her grandmother died, she went to live with the family of a friend of hers called Ward and was closer to the Ward girls than to her own sisters. She also had a friend in Dublin, Greta, who was a children's nurse for an extremely wealthy Catholic family in Dartry. These people's money was matched by their religious zeal. Greta visited my mother every week, always bringing food and second-hand clothes and shoes for me and my sisters, with her employer's blessing. We were always very well-dressed and never short of shoes or warm clothes like some of the other children on Kilfenora. Greta also brought what were then exotic fruits, like white currants, that we would never have otherwise seen.

My mother had to be creative with her cooking. She wanted to make sure her children ate nutritious food and enough of it but she was severely limited by what she could afford. I would know immediately when I came home from school if she was cooking anything with meat – usually pig's tails or feet, the gubeens, as they were called. You could get pigs' tails and feet at the butcher's for just a few pence and it didn't matter to us that they were supposedly the unsavoury parts of the animal. The smell was gorgeous and we ate every last morsel of meat, fat and dripping. We used to love it when our mother made champ, a traditional Northern Ireland dish, mashed potatoes with onions and parsley mixed through it. Today a popular version of the recipe is colcannon, mash with cabbage or kale mixed in, but my mother mightn't have been able to afford the cabbage, so she improvised, musician-like, with what was available to her. The champ was always served with a hole in the middle, with a lovely melted mass of buttery lava in a volcano of comfort food.

The one advantage that my mother had in being on her own was that she was the queen of her castle. She could invite friends and neighbours over whenever she pleased and never had to worry, as some other women did, that it would upset the man of the house. She met a lovely woman from an adjacent road at the shops and became friendly with her, inviting her back to our house for tea and biscuits several times. The woman obviously began to feel that she should return the favour by inviting my mother to her place. While they sat in the immaculate kitchen, the woman had a sweeping brush she kept banging against the table leg and along the skirting board. When my mother asked what she was doing, apples bloomed on her cheeks as she cast her eyes down in shame. She replied that her husband was upstairs in bed and if he didn't hear her working, he'd come downstairs with a belt.

Even as a young boy, I was consciously aware that the women on my street got a shit deal. As an altar boy I heard a priest telling a young bride and groom immediately after their wedding ceremony, 'Won't you have as many as you can.' My mother's reply when I told her what I'd heard was, 'But they won't keep them,' meaning it was all right for the Church to tell young couples to have scores of children when it didn't have to deal with the financial worries that burdened so many huge families. I also realised early on that while my mother went to church the same as the other women on the street, she often timed it so that she arrived late and left early. If she was listening to a radio programme and, on a very rare occasion, a priest was being criticised, a satisfied smile would play at the corner of her mouth.

There was a priest at St Agnes's church, where I was an altar boy, who was a friend of my family's, on my father's side. One Sunday, the other altar boys, had gone off on an outing and I was serving the Masses myself. After serving three Masses, I was tired and, being quite small, I stumbled with the book. The priest dragged the book roughly out of my hands and chided me, humiliating me in front of the whole congregation.

I always remember the stupidity of my blessing myself first. I made the Sign of the Cross and then I told him to fuck off and I left the altar. 'In the name of the Father and the Son and the Holy Ghost…fuck off.' I legged it home, with the priest following immediately on a bicycle. I think he probably finished the Mass before he started his pursuit but I'm not positive about that. I knew that if I had come from any other family, I would have been in for the hiding of my life, with the priest right there in the house, watching. Instead, my mother listened to the priest's side of the story. Then she listened to my side of the story. She told me that I owed the priest an apology, which I offered grudgingly, unable to meet the priest's eye. Then she told the priest that he owed me an apology.

He was devastated. At the same time, he knew he couldn't really refuse, especially now that my mother had undermined the whole point of his little staged drama – reinforcing his own authority. My mother was satisfied, told us there was a pair of us in it, asked us to shake hands and made us a cup of tea. That's one of the things I loved best about my mother – her instinctive and unfailing sense of fairness. It wasn't long after this that I decided to take my altar boy services elsewhere, to the convent instead of the church, which was probably best for all concerned.

When I became an altar boy in St Agnes's convent, I was entitled to eat breakfast there every morning. Whatever about spiritual nourishment, it was a great advantage physically because it meant that I got an egg every morning instead of only on Sundays. At the breakfast table at home, I noticed that I always got the biggest egg – I had never been as healthy as my twin sister or my other two sisters. It upset me to be singled out and eventually I started swapping the plates around when my mother's back was turned.

In my mid-teens I realised that the whole idea of Confession was somewhat arbitrary. One day, I went into the confessional with the oldest, most conservative priest in the parish and started as usual. 'Bless me father...' I told the priest how I had sinful thoughts about a girl and how I had touched her knickers.

'Do you promise not to do it again?' the priest asked sternly.

'No,' I said truthfully. I thought it better not to add, 'I'll probably do it tomorrow.'

'Then I can't absolve you,' the priest said.

I left the confessional, walked a few feet to the next empty confessional, blessed myself and said to the priest inside, 'Father X won't absolve me.'

The new judgement was delivered swiftly. 'He's getting a bit bothered,' the priest replied. 'Five Our Fathers, ten Hail Marys, go in peace.'

The year was 1950 and at the age of fourteen, I had just been expelled from Synge Street. Since I'd always been handy around the house as a boy, technical school seemed like a good choice and I spent the next two years at Bolton Street Tech doing my Group Cert. On one of my first days there I came across identical twins who were each at least one and half stone heavier and six inches taller than I was. I was always fabulously small, weighing in at around six stone ten in my teens and only reaching seven stone ten in my early twenties, around the time of my wedding. My bride was about the same weight, slight herself, causing one of the (surprisingly more senior) Kilfenora neighbours to observe on the day of our wedding, 'There'll be some rattling of bones tonight!'

I'm convinced that my small size has occasionally saved me from more physical harm than if I'd been bigger, because fellows probably figured I wasn't actually worth hitting. I encountered the identical twins, Syl and Dermot Collins, giving another student a hard time and told them, brashly but matter-of-factly, that I'd sort them myself if they didn't stop. I knew that they could have levelled me with a dig, or rather, half a dig each, but it was much more difficult for them to fight doubled over with laughter at the idea of someone my size challenging them. Syl and Dermot's mother had been a midwife for years and as children they'd tell other children that if they wanted a baby of their own, they could get one for sixpence, a racket that never quite got off the ground. Mrs Collins was strictly religious, once, according to legend, kneeling down to pray in the middle of delivering a baby because the six o'clock Angelus bell had just tolled. In years to come, Syl would find that being one of my best friends involved a lot of watching my back during various escapades and that it could, at times, be genuinely dangerous.

I did a general studies programme at Bolton Street and in addition to Irish, English, Maths and Science, I learned a lot about practical subjects like mechanics and heat, electricity, carpentry and plumbing. After two years there and a good Group Cert, I was off to an apprenticeship as a welder, fitter and turner. The country was in dire straits economically, though, and the company closed down, which took me to a job making gates and railings for a man who overworked and underpaid me.

I did something then that I find it impossible to talk about today for more than thirty seconds without laughing. In 1955, I joined the Irish Army.

2

A JOURNEY

'Gunner Crummey, number 802401. In laundry, one pair of underpants, otherwise, kit complete and ready for inspection, sir.' It must have been a rush of blood to the head that caused me to sign up for the army, because if there was ever a man who was exactly the opposite of what the army was looking for, it was me.

It was totally crazy, joining the army. I mean, the madness. I came home one day and said to my mother, 'I joined the army today.' That's the amount of thought that went into it. Aside from the fact that I was not the type to submit unquestioningly to the commands of authority figures, I lacked a certain seriousness of purpose that the army desired among young recruits. Most of the young recruits, though, were direct from industrial and reform schools and had only joined in the first place for a wage, meals and a place to sleep. I found them lovely men and got on well with just about everyone, with the exception of my lieutenant, Officer Clancy.

I loved the army training. I'd always been desperate at most organised sports but running was another story. I had the perfect lightweight sort of build for distance running and although I never had much finesse, I did have great endurance. I liked to push myself and while I was in the army I signed up for as many races as I could to avoid being in the barracks all the time. So I was well able to handle the physical demands involved. It was the rules and regulations, paired with my lieutenant's sense of importance, that I found absurd.

You'd have thought that if there was another world war, Ireland was going to win it, when it was obvious to anyone with any sense that the Irish army should be nothing but a peace-keeping force. We're not capable of going to war at any time. I found that Lieutenant Clancy was quite impressed with himself and I couldn't resist messing with someone who took himself so seriously, even if it was my officer. One night the corporal who was supposed to be leading the regiment in midnight practice manoeuvres got drunk, so I was sent out as the leader instead. For a laugh, I and a few of the others decided to make a total mess of it and everyone got killed in the first ambush. Clancy went mad! I wasn't a bad shot myself but after nearly blowing the leg off the observation post in Kilbride during grenade-throwing practice, I realised my combat skills were quite limited.

I managed to get a gold Fáinne award while I was in the army – a prestigious recognition, by exam, of fluency in the Irish language. I did it mostly to spite Clancy, who had set up a group of six soldiers to study Irish in preparation for the exam. I had not been one of those invited to sit the exam but I was in the barracks one day when I saw the six walk by in their best uniforms. I asked where they were going. When they told me they were off to take the exam, I jumped into line behind them like a youngster tagging along after older brothers, not entirely welcome. Clancy saw me, fixed me with the same kind of glare most people reserve for rats and cockroaches and told me to go back because I wasn't in the group. But I knew it was an open competition and I didn't have to be 'in the group' to sit the exam. I went in and got the gold Fáinne. The phrase, 'Fuck off, Clancy,' came to mind. I'd like to say the years have dulled my satisfaction at winning that particular round but when I tell the story, I find they haven't.

During my year or so of service, my language must have been particularly foul, because I was told by a commanding officer that it was disgraceful. In the army, where everyone cursed constantly, that was something. I also managed to lose most of my teeth. Someone was having a rough fight and, attempting to sidestep it, I caught an army boot square in the mouth, scattering teeth everywhere like white pebbles. But it wasn't until I started having blackouts that it became clear that my days in the army were numbered. I had done my 'passing out' parade (which in my case had a double meaning) that signified I had completed my training. Shortly afterwards, I was sent for and told I was being discharged for being under the army's physical standards due to the mysterious blackouts, the source of which I never discovered. It was a moot point anyway, because I never suffered from them again once I was out of the army. The discharge suited me down to the ground because I knew I had only joined in a moment of madness in the first place.

In the year that I was in the army, I hadn't missed an economic boom. It was 1956, jobs were still scarce and my next move wasn't all that obvious. In the mean time, there were the dances. St Paul's club in Mount Argus, the Passionist monastery in Kimmage, was the ultimate social scene for young adults in the area. Mount Argus had been the centre of my social life since the age of thirteen, when boys were eligible to join the confraternity. It was so popular that we told lies about our age to get in. The church would be jammed on the first Tuesday of every month with young teenagers singing hymns at the top of their lungs.

The confraternity at Mount Argus wasn't lacking for members but there were still quite a few boys who couldn't pass the Bower Cinema on Sundrive Road, which was on the way to Mount Argus, without buckling under the temptation to go to the flicks instead. On confraternity nights, Father Paul Mary C.P. from Mount Argus would go up to the cinema and do nothing but sit on his bike outside the entrance as the boys walked by, with a friendly but firm countenance. His eyebrows were so lovely and bushy they could have been used to sweep the floor. Not one boy had the nerve to pass the priest on his bicycle to get a ticket, heading instead, eyes downcast, towards the church.

I couldn't say anything but good things about the Mount Argus Passionists. I think they prepared us for life in many ways. The Passionists were a constant, kind and caring influence; the polar opposite of my experiences with most of the Christian Brothers. They were also human and they showed their human side to the boys. The older boys in the area regularly gambled over cards in the streets on a Sunday. Father Anselm C.P., a bit of a man-about-town, who wore his cap to one side, covering his eye, would often cycle up to play a hand. If the cops came and they scarpered, the cops would pick up the money and keep it. If one boy stopped and picked up the money, he was prosecuted for gambling on the street – but at least he got to keep the money. There was one day on Kilfenora when the cops came and everyone ran except one boy, Frank Murphy. The cops asked him why he hadn't run and he told them he had a bad leg. They told him to pick up the money, so he did. By the time the cop looked up from his note-pad, pencil poised to take Murphy's name, the boy was nowhere to be seen, having undergone a miraculous healing that would have been the envy of the saints.

The priests who organised the Mount Argus confraternity also ran a roads football league which was immensely popular. I was a useless footballer but I was always there, even if I was only carrying the ball. I lived for it. I would usually be put in the game if my team was sure to get beaten anyway but there were also some brilliant footballers who got their start at Mount Argus who went on to become professionals. To this day, I sometimes visit former Mount Argus confraternity fellow-members and find we can still rehash the details of particular matches we played.

I'm not sure if the people of Harold's Cross, Larkfield, Kimmage and Crumlin are aware now of the major social contribution made by the priests of Mount Argus. They were just great people and they were mates.

When I was a boy, it had all been about the matches but when I became an adult, the Saturday night dances were the highlight of the week. You weren't allowed to dance close to your girlfriend or anything and after we had drunk our minerals, everybody in the hall would kneel down and say three decades of the Rosary so your chances of getting lucky with a girl were minute. There were always observers at the dances too, all members of the dance committee, to make sure that nothing too untoward was happening between the boys and the girls. I was on the committee and my future wife, Evelyn, was the secretary.

Strict as the dance rules seemed and watchful as the eyes of the committee were, St Paul's was the only place the boys and girls of Kimmage and the surrounding areas could get together every week. For that reason alone, the dances were astoundingly popular. Over the years, the number of my friends and neighbours who met their partner at St Paul's, married and lived long and happy lives, proves that the dances were a phenomenally successful method of matchmaking.

I used to meet Evelyn at the dances but I also knew her before then because she lived on an adjacent street to Kilfenora, Bangor Road. I have always had a fabulous love for women, that probably began when I met my twin sister in the womb. From the time I was fifteen, I wanted to be married. In a strange reversal of one of the most widely-accepted stereotypes of the ages, I probably scared more than my fair share of girls away by bringing up marriage by the third date.

Pat Cullen was my first love. Pat wasn't the proverbial girl-next-door on Kilfenora but she was close enough to catch my attention. My heart literally used to miss a beat if I even saw her crossing the street. The first gift I ever bought for a girl was a daily Missal that I gave Pat for her birthday, which she still has. She was as religious as everyone else on Kilfenora and I used to love to catch a glimpse of her wearing the blue cape that signified her membership in the Children of Mary, a pious sorority that was very strong in schools and youth clubs at the time. I'd follow her up to Mass just to get to look at her there in line with all 'Mary's' other children.

Pat, like most of the other girls on the street, went to work as a young teenager and when the girls she worked with talked about things to do with boys that she didn't know about, she asked me. She always called me Crummey. She'd come home and say, 'Crummey, at work today the girls were talking about French kissing. Will you show me what that is?' Although it was obviously a burden for me to demonstrate romantic activities to the love of my life, I obliged. I'd show her what it was. It was just so innocent. We hadn't a clue – the blind leading the blind.

Pat was always friendly to me but that was the extent of her feelings. Her mother, Mrs Cullen, was one of my favourite Kilfenora women. She was also the resident matchmaker, or at least she fancied herself to be one. Some time in my teens when I was doing a line with another girl and I'd be coming down Kilfenora after walking her home, I'd see the curtains in Cullens' front window moving. Seconds later, Evelyn Ormsby would appear down the passage with the impression of Mrs Cullen's handprint fresh on the back of her blouse.

I already knew I liked Evelyn very much when I decided to go to Australia in 1956. Many of the young men from Kilfenora had already gone out on 'assisted passage', which meant their fare was ridiculously low, around ten pounds. In return, they were to work on the railways once they got to Australia. I was in the second batch of young men from Kilfenora to make the journey, which included my neighbours Harry Eastman and Noel Kenny. I didn't qualify for the assisted passage because I had missed the application deadline and the fare was £178, a lot of money in those days. My mother put it up for me. Noel Kenny was also ineligible for the assisted passage and my mother lent him money for his ticket, too, on the condition that he would send it back to her once he got a job in Australia. There was absolutely no question between either of them but that he would honour his word and pay back the money. That's just the way people on Kilfenora were.

The ship that Harry, Noel and I were booked on was the *Large Bay*. Evelyn, Pat Cullen and other well-wishers from Kilfenora came to Dún Laoghaire harbour to say good-bye. Back in the 1950s, young men who went off to Australia were usually gone for a long time – sometimes for good. It wasn't just a gap year. For one thing, work was plentiful there.

Noel and I had a cabin to ourselves and Harry shared with a crowd of others, including a young man our age from Tipperary called Donal. I was busy chatting up Donal's sister, Mary. The siblings, along with the other young men and women on the ship from the Irish countryside, were naïve in a way that my mates and I could never have been, having grown up on Kilfenora. When I asked Mary if she wanted to go up to the deck with me, she said bluntly, 'You mean for swapping spits?'

Mary may have been innocent but she knew enough to come to us for help when she and her brother were being bullied by another Tipperary man on the ship. Harry, Noel and I paid the bully a visit in his cabin. Harry was the toughest and most intimidating of us and told the bully that if he fancied swimming to Australia, he was going the right way about it. If he gave Donal and Mary any more grief, overboard he'd be going. Donal couldn't quite understand how it was that three strangers from Dublin would look after him but he still remembered it more than thirty years later when, as a self-made millionaire, he invited Evelyn and me to his estate in Leeds for a visit.

As the journey wore on, rumours flew around the boat that a third world war was starting, which was why the *Large Bay* wasn't going through the Suez Canal as originally planned. It was actually the Suez War that had started and the *Large Bay* was diverted to Las Palmas, where my friends and I went to Mass in the cathedral. Then it was on to Capetown, where I took a cable car to the top of Table Mountain and played a game of chess there. From Capetown the *Large Bay* went on to Durban, then crossed the Indian Ocean into Freemantle. Six weeks after leaving Dún Laoghaire, we were on Australian soil. I went to live with some of the boys from the first Kilfenora wave, Joe Cullen (Pat Cullen's brother) and Bud Fagan.

It turned out that our intervening on Donal's behalf wasn't finished. Donal was set to work on the railways, Mary was looking for a job and an aunt had picked them up at the seaport and arranged to take them in. But the aunt was taking their money for rent and giving them a very hard time, so Mary contacted me again, even though I was living in a different part of Melbourne. I rounded up the lads and paid a visit to the aunt: other living arrangements were made for both Donal and Mary.

The abundance of work allowed us great freedom because we could walk off of a job one day, go travelling to another city and find a new job when we returned to Melbourne. I worked at all kinds of odd jobs in Australia, including making chain wire for fences and brushing sawdust up a shoot in a furniture factory. I hitchhiked to Sydney, where I met my cousin Billie Sugden (a girl) and my Aunt May and Uncle James, a brother and sister of my mother's, for the first time. I also went to the 1956 Olympics, and I was in the stand when Ronnie Delaney won his gold medal for Ireland in the 1500-metre race. I remember seeing Delaney make his final break for the finish – you could see, from the stands, that he could feel the swing of the gold around his neck – and the rising excitement that we were witnessing an Irish win.

The whole time I was writing to Evelyn, with whom I had realised, somewhat startlingly, that I was madly in love. Even with all the Kilfenora natives in Melbourne, I recognised my homesickness and lovesickness for what they were. It was obvious that I wasn't settling in the same way the others were.

The ship I booked on to come home was the *Aurelia*, an Italian vessel. Above all the Italian voices when the boat was pulling out of Melbourne, I heard a broad Dublin accent behind me saying, 'And what part of Dublin are you from?' I turned to see a tall, lanky man a few years older than me whose name was Padraic Mac Ionnraic. We remained friends until the day he died and we disagreed on absolutely everything. We had nothing in common. Padraic was from Glasnevin, a posher area than Kimmage, and he was a gentleman to the fingertips. He was also returning home because he was madly in love and couldn't stand to be away any longer from the object of his affection, Cáit O'Connor.

One of my favourite words that can actually be used in polite company is 'aggro,' which is, in essence, a tolerable level of aggravation that in my case is usually mixed with a good laugh and some excitement. There was plenty of aggro on the *Aurelia*. We discovered on the first day of the voyage that the food on the ship was dismal and the standards of cleanliness disgraceful, so Padraic, who was a better writer, drafted a letter of complaint to the ship's captain and I signed it. We both knew I'd be better at the vocal, 'having a go' side of things. Within an hour of handing it in to the purser's office, I was called up and brought before the captain, where I told him I'd be giving a story about the ship's condition to the papers when I got back to Dublin. Within an hour, the smell of disinfectant all over the vessel was poisonous. For the rest of the journey, everyone got their meals at the dining table except for me, whose dinner would come out a few minutes later served on a silver platter with a shiny dome top, complete with potatoes cooked to order. I think it was the potatoes that really pushed Padraic's buttons. He was going mad. 'I wrote the bleeding letter,' he said in astonishment to no one in particular. 'The boy only signed it. The boy put his name up front.'

I also learned that while Padraic had many lovely qualities, being helpful in a fight was not one of them. One night when we were watching a film in the lounge, there was a commotion out on the deck. We rushed out to see a man brandishing a steel chair, bashing everyone around him, going berserk. He was a big man but I was used to challenging people who were bigger than me, since that included just about everyone. I never saw myself as small or, at least, I never let that dissuade me from stepping in and stopping a fight. Now it occurs to me that I probably looked like a parakeet chasing an Alsatian, oblivious of how ridiculous I must have seemed. In this case, I used my agility to my advantage and jumped over the arc of the swinging chair in a sort of half-tackle on top of the crazy man but I wasn't really strong enough to hold him down. I had the guy by the hair, while Padraic was gently trying to sit on his legs like a refined diner who has just found something unpleasant on his chair and can't quite bring himself to lower his arse. The master-at-arms and the crew came out to the rescue and after that, we were the heroes of the ship.

But the excitement of the voyage wasn't over. One day while at Mass on the ship, I saw a man bless himself and walk up the stairs to the next deck. A few minutes later there was an announcement over the loudspeakers in Italian, causing exclamations from the congregation. The Italian man beside me turned to me and said, 'Man overboard.' The man I'd seen walking up to the next deck had thrown himself into the Indian Ocean, which on that day was as still as a bowl of soup. Padraic held me by the legs and lowered me over the side of the ship so I could get a photograph with my little box camera of the lifeboats bringing the man back to the ship. The man overboard had survived the fall and being in the water but he had hit his leg on the side of the ship as he went down and broken it, causing an embolism from which he died shortly afterwards. Padraic and I were excited about the prospect of seeing a burial at sea, maybe because funerals were always such a good day out on Kilfenora. But because the death had been a suicide the head office ordered the ship to bring the body back to the port at Messina. The crew had to store the body in the ship's refrigerator. Every time we got a meal after that we'd say, 'We got his toe today,' or, 'That's definitely fingers.'

I arrived back in Dublin just in time for my sister Marie's wedding on 1 July 1957, exactly one week before my twenty-first birthday.

3

London Bus Days

I was back on Kilfenora with my mother and blissfully happy to be near Evelyn again but jobs were still scarce. I ended up at Glenabbey Textiles and the upside for me was that the bulk of Glenabbey's product line was ladies' underwear. I bought the slightly flawed factory seconds from the company and set up a little side trade for myself selling slips, underskirts and knickers, which I would cart to the regular Saturday night dances at St Paul's and sell to the girls coming out of the hall. To round out my selection of merchandise, I also used to bring along nylons I bought from a wholesaler. Evelyn would wait for me while I set up shop outside, not at all put off by her unorthodox suitor/salesman.

Far from being bashful about selling unmentionables to girls I knew very well, I had a great time as a merchant outside the dance hall. I was a hustler. I had some great laughs and it was a way of earning a few extra shillings. My first love, Pat Cullen, was working at the De La Rue money-printing factory in Clonskeagh and she brought my goods in for the girls there. She was like an agent and she even kept an account book for me as she sold my knickers and slips. Having a captive market was a big help. They were great girls, the way they rallied around.

I was a member of the Our Lady, Cause of Our Joy branch of the Legion of Mary committee that organised the Saturday dances. One of the jobs committee members were charged with was the manning of the back gates at Mount Argus at the end of the dances so that the teenagers couldn't take a shortcut through the grounds on their way home, disturbing the priests who were already in bed. I volunteered for gate duty one night and Evelyn came along too. I didn't waste any time working my charms on Evelyn, until I felt a tap on my shoulder. I turned around to a priest's disapproving question, 'What are you doing?'

Evelyn froze. But I said, 'What do you think I'm doing? I'm courting. Now if you go away and leave me alone, I'll continue.' And instead of me panicking, he panicked. He ran down Loder Park like a blue-arsed fly.

Some girls were shyer than others about buying underwear and they'd send their friends over to me instead of approaching me themselves. When I'd see them the following week, I'd ask if they were wearing their new purchases. Somehow the transactions were never as awkward as they could have been and eventually some of the girls started coming up directly to my house to buy nylons instead of waiting until Saturday night at the dances.

I didn't have the money to buy Evelyn the things that Glenabbey sold in perfect condition but I was a consummate romantic and I still liked lavishing little surprises on her. One of the most popular items from Glenabbey was 'baby doll' pyjamas, which were two-piece sets of shorts and a lightweight top to match. I got the pattern and after the workers had gone home one night, I sewed the pyjamas for Evelyn on an interlocking machine. I wrapped them up in a bit of newspaper and brought them over to her house. She was out for the night, so I left them with her mother.

Big mistake.

To say that Mrs Ormsby disapproved of her daughter's relationship with me would be like saying that Juliet's family thought she could do better than Romeo. On this particular night, she was very interested to know just what the troublemaker – or, as I was known by most of the neighbours, the 'little mouth' – was doing giving Evelyn sleepwear.

By the time we had our wedding ceremony, I was nearly twenty-five and had been working in London for almost two years as a bus driver. Like so many of the young men from Kilfenora and all over Ireland who had gone off to Australia to find work, I now found myself joining the ranks of Irish emigrants to London for the same reason. If I wanted to get married, I knew I needed to save money and I couldn't do that on my pay from Glenabbey.

The problem was that although lots of Irish men knew there were decent jobs with London Transport, one of the requirements as part of a job application was a letter of reference from a previous employer. Since so many of them hadn't been able to find work in Dublin – which was the reason they were going to London in the first place – this was a conundrum. A local family of barbers, the Roches, who owned their own ladies and gents hairdressing salon on Lower Kimmage Road, came to the rescue. There was a disproportionately high number of London bus drivers and conductors who had been exemplary employees of brothers Fergus and Brendan Roche, according to the letters signed by them in support of the young men of Kimmage and the surrounding areas.

I was among the crop of proud former barbers. I started out as a bus conductor and after three months went on to become a bus driver, which paid eleven pounds and four shillings per week, four shillings more than conductors were paid. At seven stone ten, I was the lightest bus driver London Bus had ever employed, according to the records in their Peckham medical office. I was probably also the first and the last to attempt and successfully execute a three-point turn in Oxford Street during rush hour, a feat that made the papers the next day. Although I missed Evelyn, I channelled all my romantic notions about our wedding day into energy for extra work. I took as many hours as I could of the unlimited overtime London Transport offered its employees and sent Evelyn all the money I had left over each week from my living expenses, which I kept to a bare minimum.

From the very beginning, Evelyn was the one who was much better at finance and budgets than me. I would have happily ignored all money issues. Evelyn was puzzled when an old Kilfenora neighbour came home from London for a visit and told her he was making fabulous money, much more than me, in 'the travel industry'. She asked me if I could look into finding some kind of a job with these wages myself to speed up our marriage plans. I wasn't against the idea but I was puzzled. What specific job could this man be working at that paid so well? The mystery was sorted out a short while later, when I saw him on another bus, working as a conductor. Later on, Kilfenora natives knew him as 'Paddy the liar' for the fibs he constantly told.

I loved being a London bus driver. At the time, London Transport was short of employees, so they were particularly good to the ones they had. The inspectors soon realised that if they needed a first or a last bus covered, I was their man, because I was always on time and always looking for the hours. My love for the job was also obvious.

I worked with one clippy from Newcastle in County Down, Theresa Paul. Her lover Charlie was a driver on the one-five-nines and she used to ask me to time my bus to jump Charlie's at the Oval so she could lean off the back of it and kiss him through the sliding window, much to the amusement of the passengers. Theresa's case proved that I really was a romantic to the bone, because I couldn't resist loaning her the money she needed to marry Charlie. I was just married myself by the time she needed the loan and Evelyn and I still had very little money but I knew what it felt like to be waiting and saving.

As much as I loved my job – and it was the first time in my life I had a job I loved – my years in London put me in some extraordinary circumstances. In one instance, I found myself in exactly the wrong place at the wrong time. In another, I missed the one chance I would ever have to get to know my father before I even had time to recognise that chance for what it was.

After my three months as a conductor, I was keen to become a driver. One day, when I had just begun going out on practice runs with an instructor, I was driving toward Stockwell station when I saw a dark blur out of the corner of my eye. I hit the anchors hard. I hadn't been going fast so I was able to stop in the length of a bus – but it was too late. My front wheel had just gone over the chest of a seventeen year-old boy. The boy had been on his motorbike, hit a stationary milk truck beside my bus and had been thrown forward, directly into my path. I stopped and just sat for a minute. 'He's dead,' I said finally, to no one in particular.

'Jesus,' I heard Fred Porthard, the bus instructor, say from behind me. I took out the saw that was in place over the driver's head in every bus back then, got out of the cab and cut away the lifeguard.

He was right behind the front wheel. I got underneath the bus, said a prayer for him and he died.

Crowds had gathered and the fire brigade arrived. Incredibly, I heard one man from the crowd say, 'Ah, fuck it, push him into the side of the road and drive off.' This didn't help my state of mind. Fred Porthard was extremely nice to me, trying to reassure me in the immediate aftermath of the accident. The body was taken away and according to procedure, the bus had to be removed so that it could be checked for problems. London Transport's policy was to get a driver involved in an accident right back into another bus, which was supposed to ease the nerves about getting back on the road by denying the driver any time to dwell on things. When I got to Stockwell station, the nearest one to the accident, they gave me another bus and told me to take it up to my own station on Brixton Hill. The distance seemed three times its length that day.

When we got to Brixton Hill, the inspectors came over to me

and put their arms around me. They were really good people. Fred Porthard and I had to go up to the canteen with another inspector to fill out an accident report. Another employee, Dessie Noone, passed by and said to me sideways, 'Howya, killer?'

They jumped on him. I could tell they were going to bash him for me. I said, 'No, no, that's my mate!' They said, 'Jesus, don't show us your enemies.' Dessie was just a messer and I knew not to take him seriously.

Dealing with the accident was harder for me because Evelyn and my family were far away. It also added much more stress to my upcoming road test because I was worried my examiner would have heard about the accident. The instructor I was working with reassured me that the examiners wouldn't know about anything. There were two examiners everyone knew about, one called Greene, the other called Wakeland. If Greene was your examiner, you knew to drive like hell and Wakeland was the opposite – you drove very carefully and gave nobody a fright.

There were two others taking their tests on the same day as me. I wanted to get my test over with, so I volunteered to go first and the instructor said reassuringly to me, 'Remember, your examiner doesn't know anything.'

I was expecting to see either Greene or Wakeland but instead I was paired with someone I'd never met before, who turned out to be Mr Boyle, the head instructor.

The minute I saw that I said to myself, 'My bollocks he doesn't know.'

All three of us had to do basic reversing and manoeuvring before the road test and the one thing I had a knack for was reversing a bus well, so my test got off to a good start. As I was getting ready to go out on to the road, I heard Mr Boyle say to Mr Porthard, 'This is the guy who had the fatal, isn't it?'

The road test was mostly uneventful. Everyone knew that if they were told to go upstairs once they had finished their driving it meant they had failed but if they were told to come inside with the examiner, he would ask them the rules of the road while the others finished their road tests. I was called inside and a while later I saw the second man who had taken his road test heading up the stairs. The third man hit another bus out on the road and that was the end of his test.

The coroner's findings indicated that there was nothing at all I could have done to avoid the accident. He told me I had just been unfortunate but that didn't make me feel any less terrible. I found out later that the boy who had died was an only child from Morden in Surrey.

I had had no contact with my father since he had left the family permanently when I was about nine years old. But while in London, I had heard through some of my aunts and uncles in Dublin that he had recently moved to the city, after living in Birmingham for years. My sources also had an address for my father, in Finsbury Park. It was just up to me to knock on his door, if I wanted.

I was a full-fledged driver now and I worked with a young clippy from Arklow, Margaret Byrne, who was a great girl. One night after we'd finished work, I said to Margaret, 'Come on, we'll go over to Finsbury Park and see if we can find my father.' I almost always prefer to take someone else along for whatever adventure I start. This one, although uniquely sensitive, was no exception – in fact, I really wanted someone else for company.

My father had one rented room in a house and when we rang for him and he came down the stairs, I could tell he was stunned to see me. What could he have been thinking? I said, 'Hello, how are you?' and invited him for a drink. I found him articulate, an interesting conversationalist and good company. It wasn't at all like the movies where the son confronts the deserting father and they unload years of hard feelings and hurt on each other. Obviously, since it was my first time to be with him in years and years, I was trying hard to be polite. My father told us that he was working as a fitter and Margaret and I arranged to meet him another night after we all finished work. Then Margaret offered to cook a Sunday roast for me in my flat and suggested I ask my father to join us. You can see what I mean about her being great.

The three of us had dinner and a chat while I began to put together some little parts of my father's life, hoping to fit the pieces into a complete picture. I realised he was a member of the Ancient Order of Buffaloes – the poor man's Freemasons. He played chess and bridge, like I did. He had spent most of his life after he left Dublin in Aston, Birmingham. But I wasn't ready to ask any of the big questions yet. Maybe I just wanted to get to know him first as a man, cautiously, through some of the small, everyday things that, in the end, made up who my father really was. I was starting to find out about him for the first time as a young twenty-something, and awkwardness was inevitable. We were like strangers who happened to share family members and a few dim memories. This process of getting to know him was much more difficult than starting from scratch with new people, which has always been very easy for me.

At the end of the Sunday dinner, my father and I arranged to meet again the following Tuesday after I had finished my shift. But when I checked my post on Tuesday there was a note from my father saying he was very sorry that he couldn't meet me that night because he had been admitted to the Whittington Hospital in Highgate. The note went on to say, very politely, that he didn't expect me to visit him but he would be very honoured if I did.

When I think about it now, I regret that I didn't go into the garage right then and tell them I had a family problem I needed to take care of. I still don't know why I didn't – they would have immediately cancelled my bus and given me the day off, because they were really good about family emergencies. But the card hadn't said anything about what the problem was and for all I knew, he could have been in for an ingrown toenail. We had seen each other just a few days before and he had seemed fine.

At about six-thirty that night, Margaret and I hopped on the tube and headed over to Whittington Hospital. At the front desk, they told me the ward my father was in but when I walked in, I didn't see anyone who resembled him. Then I saw one empty bed. The beginning of one of those awful sick, sinking feelings twisted and spiralled downwards through my stomach. A nurse asked me if I needed help and I told her who I was looking for, even though I already knew what the answer would be. She asked me to step into the matron's office, where the matron told me she was terribly sorry but that my father had just died.

I had hoped to ease in with him and then come to the parts about what went wrong, without being nasty, because too much water had passed under the bridge and I don't believe in being nasty to anybody. The only person you harm with bitterness is yourself.

There's a famous quote I heard once about how every man tries either to live up to his father's expectations or make up for his father's mistakes. I wish I had known my father well enough to understand what his expectations of me might have been. The sadness I felt over his death wasn't really because he was my daddy. I was so frustrated, wondering what kind of life we might all have had together and hating the fact that I could never know.

I was concerned that my father hadn't seen a priest before he died but through the half-opened door of the matron's office, I saw the plain, crisp uniform of a Catholic priest. Now, in this moment, there was comfort for me in the familiarity of these sombre hues. I went out and asked him if he was a Roman Catholic priest and when he said yes, I asked him if he could give my father a blessing. Later I found out the priest was in the Passionist order, the same as the priests at my beloved Mount Argus in Kimmage. This alone made me feel better because however my opinions about religion may have evolved, I've always had a deep respect for Mount Argus and the Passionists there.

When I went back to my father's room in Finsbury Park to collect his belongings, all his worldly possessions fitted inside one kit bag. I found that sad but not surprising. The man I had known so little about had left barely anything behind to mark his existence. He had a few medals from the Ancient Order of Buffaloes, the British Army and the IRA, an unusual assortment in any circumstances.

I took charge of planning the funeral. I rang my mother, sisters and aunts and uncles in Dublin. I used most of the money I had been saving for my wedding to Evelyn to cover the funeral costs and my father was buried at Highgate Cemetery. He had died of lung cancer. My sister Marie and her husband Des flew over for the funeral, as did my father's brothers. But my mother stayed home. She arranged for a Mass in Mount Argus, which she attended.

One year when I was very young and my father was away in the war, the army notified my mother that he would be on the radio. My family and most of Kilfenora Road crowded around our radio at seven o'clock on the morning of the broadcast. We waited through a few of the other soldiers speaking, the children all fidgeting and impatient, for so long that we thought he wasn't coming on. Then the announcement crackled through: 'Now we have an ambulance driver, Frank Crummey, from Dublin.'

He just said he was doing well and he hoped we were all happy. And there were tears. In one way or another and whether or not he always meant to, my father spent his whole life far enough away from us to remain just out of our reach.

4

MEETINGS AND BRAWLS

Dessie Noone, another former Dublin 'barber' like me who went to work for London Bus, had narrowly missed being pounced on by our co-workers in the canteen of the bus garage for his flip reaction to my accident behind the wheel. But as I had said then, Dessie *was* my mate. Not only was he my mate, he was my roommate in the cramped bedsit we shared in Brixton as I saved up my money for my wedding to Evelyn, starting over again from scratch after covering my father's funeral expenses.

Dessie had strange ways of demonstrating his friendship and 'quirky' would be an exceptionally kind description of him as a roommate. Our colleague in London Bus, Les Hamerton, doubled as our landlord and lived downstairs. One night, he heard loud scuffling from the room upstairs and ran in to see what the problem was. Inside our room, he found me pummelling Dessie in a fight that had erupted over keeping the light turned on or switching it off. He later described the scene as that of a midget attacking a giant. It isn't hard to guess who was who.

To make things even more interesting, Dessie's girlfriend, Liz, lived one floor up from us. Liz was a nurse whom I found lovable and affectionate but she was one of the first people to teach me that someone can be lovable and affectionate without being all that reliable. One afternoon as she was going out to the shops she asked me if there was anything I needed. I gave her five pounds and a short list – tea, butter and a few other things. At a time when my weekly wage was eleven pounds, I knew I'd be owed at least four pounds back. But when Liz returned, she gave me my items and nothing else.

'Sorry, Liz, what about my change?' I asked her.

'Well, I don't know,' she stammered innocently. 'I don't have it.'

'What do you mean?' I said. 'How could that be? There's no way this could have cost the full fiver.'

Liz insisted she didn't have the change and went upstairs to her room. Dessie came home a few minutes later and Liz, obviously hearing him, called down to him. 'Desmond, come up!' her voice lilted down the stairs.

'She's calling you up to show you something she bought with my money!' I said to Dessie indignantly.

'I know,' Dessie said. Part of him must have felt sorry for me, because he added, 'You go up.'

I bounded up the stairs to find Liz standing there provocatively in matching blue knickers, suspenders and a bra. 'I couldn't leave them behind!' she said to me. 'I'll owe you for them.' Needless to say, I never got the money.

I witnessed a serious argument between the lovers some time later when Liz told Dessie she was pregnant. That ended with Liz stripping off all her clothes and running out into the street completely naked; Dessie, having just proclaimed that he wanted nothing to do with her problem, left the dramatic running after her to me. I grabbed my overcoat and dashed out into the street. People were starting to stare but I didn't know where to grab her. For one thing, she had short hair.

Not long after that, I helped Liz get settled into a home for unmarried mothers where the nun in charge could not be persuaded that I wasn't the father. Months later, when the apartment phone rang and the same nun told me that Liz had just had her baby, I said to her, 'Hold on a minute while I let the father know.' I turned to Dessie and delivered the news.

'Frank, you tell that nun to tell Liz that I love her and I want to marry her,' Dessie said.

'Did you hear that?' I said into the receiver.

Les Hamerton very generously offered to pay for the wedding reception/christening, which were to be held on the same day. Dessie's sister was supposed to be the bridesmaid/godmother but she never turned up. I grabbed my beloved clippy, Margaret, saying, 'C'mon, you're up!' and shoved her into both positions of honour.

It wasn't all happy-ever-after for Dessie and Liz. Before long, he started staying out after work, gambling and drinking. He and Liz had terrible rows. One day, he went into work to find that he had an unexpected day off. In one of the most clichéd and heart-wrenching of scenarios, he returned home to find his wife in bed with a man they had both known back in Dublin, another emigrant. Dessie threw the man and his clothes out in the front garden. He went back inside and sat down on his wife's bed, from where she was now watching him out of one scrunched-up eye. Her head was turned to the side and she sat with the covers up to her chin, bracing herself for the explosion of rage she knew was about to come. Instead, a strange, inexplicable calm descended. 'Look,' he said to his cheating wife, 'Isn't it about time we both grew up? I'm no angel and you're certainly no angel.'

From then on, as I remember it, the couple idolised each other. It was as if, after Dessie's acknowledgement that they were both behaving like children, they were able to move on with their life together and cultivate actual, genuine respect for each other. They lived like that, in happiness and relative peace, until Dessie came home from work some years later to find Liz dead in bed of what he later found out was a brain seizure.

I made other friends at London Bus who, in some ways, couldn't have been more different from the usual Paddies whom Irish emigrants in London were expected to hang around with. Although not as strong in number as the Irish, there were many black men from Jamaica and Barbados finding their way to the city and to jobs at London Bus. I could see right away that they were the underdogs and I've always liked underdogs. I was playing snooker in the recreation room of the garage one night when I gave a shot to one of my black colleagues at the end of the table, who was obviously reluctant to take it. Another Paddy from Kimmage was playing and he refused to move out of the black man's way so he could play the shot. So I hit him with a billiard cue and he moved.

At first, the black men I worked with couldn't understand a Paddy hitting another Paddy in defence of a black man. Their reactions weren't unlike that of the country boy, Donal, on the *Large Bay* to Australia who was incredulous at our protecting him. To me, a bully is a bully and the details don't matter much. After the billiard cue incident, when any of the black workers got in trouble in the garage, they always asked for me to come in and 'represent' them to the boss.

One of my favourite conductors was a man from Barbados with the honest name of Clarence Best. Clarence was tall, thin and the blackest person I had ever seen. We got on fabulously well, probably in large part because neither of us cared much for political correctness. When we went on breaks together, Clarence would say to me, 'Going to wash your hands, Chalkie?' and expect the normal answer, 'Yes and you can have a tin of shoe polish.' Clarence had been a tailor in his home country and he fixed hems on some of Evelyn's clothes.

I knew that the black conductors were especially nervous on their first day of work. By that time, they'd been told by their bosses that everything had to run very smoothly and that they had to collect fares at certain stages and at certain times. Coming from the cultures most of them came from, they weren't at all used to such strict regimentation. So I looked after them on their first days, flashing my lights at the right stages to signal where they were and shooing inspectors off the bus with a firm, 'Leave him alone, it's only his first day.' I told them that if passengers asked for directions they should give them the minimum fare and tell them to look out the window and figure out where they were for themselves. I always noticed that the black conductors would have purses bursting with coins at the end of their shifts because they were much less likely than the white conductors to ask people for smaller change. I think a lot of them remembered me. About a dozen years later when I went back to London to visit, I boarded a bus where the black driver immediately recognised me and invited me for a drink as an acknowledgement for looking after him on his first day as a conductor.

I looked after Clarence, too, but I knew our friendship wasn't enough to make him comfortable at work and in London. One day when we were working together, I looked through my window and saw several women on the street gawking after my bus. I stopped immediately to find that a woman whom I hadn't even seen had jumped off my bus, hit a pedestrian rail and rolled under the platform.

Normally, according to procedure, the conductor was supposed to take the names of witnesses in such incidents while the driver went to call an ambulance. But I thought that in Clarence's case, especially since he was so gentle and soft-spoken, it would be better to switch duties. So Clarence went off to the public phone box and I began taking down names, numbers and accounts of what had happened. A small crowd had gathered and minutes passed and then more minutes, with no sign of the ambulance. Finally, I went down to the phone box to find Clarence waiting in a long queue. 'They're all white,' he told me to explain why he hadn't pushed through to the front to report the emergency.

Although it took several years, I eventually saved the marriage money, sending it over to Evelyn faithfully every week until she wrote back to me to say it was enough.

When Evelyn and I eventually broke the news to her parents that we were engaged, it was probably all that Mrs Ormsby could do to keep from weeping openly in front of us – and not out of happiness. The word that best describes her reaction is 'devastated'. Evelyn's mother used to visit her neighbour Mrs Hughes and confide in her that she got a pain in the pit of her stomach at the thoughts of her Evelyn marrying 'that little bastard'.

But it was when Mrs Ormsby heard the date we were setting for the wedding – 17 March – that she really became distressed. We couldn't understand what the big problem was and Evelyn's mother wouldn't tell us, so we decided that if a simple date meant that much to her, we'd just push it forward a week or two to the beginning of April. It was only later that we found out that St Patrick's Day was traditionally the only day during Lent when it was acceptable for pregnant girls to get married and there was a deep-seated stigma in our parents' generation against marriage vows being exchanged on that day. We got married on 4 April 1961.

Evelyn's father was a tailor and her family was quite respectable. She was the youngest of the children. They lived on the road next to Kilfenora, one that was wider and more genteel simply for that reason. More distance between the houses on either side of the street meant that fights couldn't take place between neighbours across from one another, if only because there was more traffic. Fights were a weekly occurrence on the narrow Kilfenora, where there were no passing cars to act as moving barriers. My mother liked Evelyn very much but she was the only one who saw Evelyn as marrying 'above her station' because, of course, the woman who married 'her Frank' was a lucky woman indeed.

When word circulated on the street that we were engaged,

Evelyn walked into Twomey's, the shop that had formerly been Corcoran's, where my mother bought most of her food and odds and ends. Helena Twomey, the owner and a great friend of my mother, called her over.

'Are you Evelyn, the girl that's marrying Frank Crummey?' she asked.

Evelyn said she was.

'If you were the Blessed Virgin herself, you wouldn't be good enough for Mrs Crummey's Frank,' Miss Twomey said, not un-kindly.

Around the same time, one of Evelyn's friends, Mary Kavanagh (later O'Callaghan) stopped her in the street and said, 'Can I ask you a question?'

Evelyn said yes.

'What in the name of God do you see in Frank Crummey?' she asked.

It was enough to confuse a girl but Evelyn is sharp and she knew what she was doing. At the very least, she knew me well enough to expect her marriage to be quite different from most other girls' marriages.

I flew home to get married. In those days, passengers arriving at Dublin airport walked down the stairs attached to the planes and across the tarmac into the building. Friends and family waiting to meet them could see them from the time they stepped out of the plane and on to the stairs until they entered the airport building to go through customs. What Evelyn saw the day she met me as I arrived home for our wedding was her skinny husband-to-be crossing the tarmac jauntily with a baby in his arms and no wedding suit.

I had ordered a custom-made suit for the wedding from the famous Burton's of Brixton in London. I was measured in the shop and was excited about picking up my suit for our big day but when I went to collect it the day before my flight back home, it was a disaster – the suit was so oversized that three of me could have fit in it. I still don't know exactly what went wrong but I suppose that even though they took my measurements, they couldn't believe the tiny dimensions. I might have been better off browsing through the Communion suit section of another shop.

The baby in my arms was a more complicated matter than the suit. It was, not surprisingly, indirectly related to my roommate, Dessie Noone. The same day I discovered the suit disaster, I was in the canteen of the bus garage with Dessie and a girl Dessie knew from Dublin, to whom Dessie had just introduced me.

'Listen, can I ask you to do me a favour?' she asked me.

'What's that?' I said.

'I'm going into hospital and I've no one to mind my baby,' she said. 'Would you bring him home with you to Dublin to my mother?'

'If you're at the airport and have everything organised,' I said, 'I'll take him home.' Which is how I ended up with the infant boy in my arms on my flight home, feeding him a bottle. Evelyn, calm as the eye of a hurricane, barely batted an eye. By now, she was as used to my schemes as many other women must be to their husbands' predictability.

'Frank,' she said reasonably, once I'd told her whose baby I was carrying and where I was to deliver him, 'What are you going to do if this girl's mother tells you she wants no part of this?'

I admitted I hadn't thought of that. I started to get nervous when I went to see the mother and noticed right away that she wasn't giving any indication that she was expecting this special delivery. In fact, she wasn't even looking at the baby much. Paling now, I filled her in on her daughter's plans.

'I didn't know she had a baby!' the mother said.

Lucky for me, she recovered in a heartbeat. 'Well, never mind,' she said. 'There's a baby to be minded.'

I wasn't really worried, because that's how Dublin people are.

She wouldn't have taken it out on the baby.

'Frank,' Evelyn said, after I had successfully delivered the baby, 'how do you get yourself into these situations?'

As for my suit, Jimmy Mitten, a tailor I knew, saved the day. I went to Jimmy and said, 'I need a suit and not in a few weeks, for the day after tomorrow.'

'Let's get to work, then,' Jimmy said.

Mitten the tailor stayed up all night to finish my suit and I looked smashing on my wedding day. 'I'm in love with Evelyn today,' I said in my speech to our friends and relatives, some of whom (on Evelyn's side) were still nearly inconsolable at the thought of the match. 'But not as much as I will be in forty-five years.' In the wedding photos, Evelyn's family members all have the expressions of funeral attendees mistakenly dressed in wedding attire.

Today I reckon I missed an opportunity to make some serious money at our wedding. If I had opened a book on how long the marriage would last, I figure I could have afforded to retire in style years ago. People could have placed bets of two years, up to six, seven, eight…but I don't think anyone would have gone as high as ten.

Michael Cleary was the priest who married us and I still think it's one of the few positive things he ever did. It wasn't the end of my contact with Father Cleary: we bumped into each other years later during my career as a social worker.

After our wedding, our first stop was to the convent so the nuns could see Evelyn in her dress. She gave them the dress soon after so they could recycle the material for priests' vestments. Their reception of me was kind enough. My most serious – and public – criticisms of the Church were to come later.

Evelyn and I spent a few very happy years in London. While we were there, just a few days after we'd been married for nine months, our first baby, Elizabeth – named after my mother –

was born. I love babies and was thrilled with our lovely little girl. Sometimes if I was working a late shift, Evelyn would come out to my bus with the baby and sit behind me, waving back and forth. My colleagues loved Elizabeth too and would mind her sometimes if we wanted a night to ourselves.

Evelyn also fitted in comfortably in London, which was a big change from Dublin for her in both size and culture. Even though it was her first prolonged time away from home, she made great friends. To her, far from their stoic, 'stiff upper lip' stereotype, British people were warm and affectionate. She remembers friends of hers seeing her coming up the street for a visit and running to put the kettle on in anticipation.

Although we both loved London and I loved bus driving, when we heard that the grip of unemployment was loosening in Ireland we decided it was time to go back home. I wasn't sure yet what I would do but I did know where we'd live. Home was nowhere but Kilfenora. Evelyn, Elizabeth and I moved in with my mother, who had been on her own since the last of my sisters had left to get married.

To date, I'd been a welder, gate-maker, soldier-in-training, sawdust sweeper, independent underwear salesman and London bus driver. Second to bus driving, easily the occupation I had enjoyed the most was underwear sales. I decided to open my own shop on Sundrive Road called 'Little Eve's.' Besides the obvious, I also sold things like cardigans and drapes. The shop lasted just about a year before folding. I'm the first to admit I'm no businessman. On a very basic level, I've never been that interested in money and finances beyond the point at which I had enough to survive and support my family. If I did ever find I had surplus, like a well-meaning dog might find itself covered in burrs – by accident – I usually found someone to give it to.

Evelyn was extremely laid-back about the money situation. She knew I was a 'grafter', willing to work at practically anything. As I moved further into my twenties, it was becoming obvious that I changed jobs as easily as other men changed hats. My mother had mentioned once or twice that it was important to find a job, eventually, with a good pension scheme. My personal recurring nightmare was a scene in which I was presented with a watch and a certificate for thirty years of good service to the same company.

It was the early 1960s and my next job was in the driving seat of a taxi. Lots of friends and acquaintances thought this was a perfect job for me. Like the ideal bartenders of old, I'm a talker but I know how to listen. But I found taxi driving monotonous and an all-around lousy way of making a living. It turned out that I was much better suited to driving large vehicles full of people than small ones with just one or two.

You picked up the poshest of the posh and the lowest of the low in the taxi. They included criminals, business people, writers and movie stars. There were the women up around St Michan's, who would offer me a note in one hand and a condom in the other for me to chose between. One night I was sitting in the rank with the other drivers. It was completely dead. A woman came running over to the first taxi in the rank and asked the driver how much it would be to get to Tralee. He thought quickly of a figure, doubled it, added about half as much again and told her. She paid him straight away in cash and he was thrilled to get the exorbitant fare. About twenty minutes later, a squad car pulled up to the rank and a Garda got out and asked the drivers if any woman had tried to get a taxi in the last little while. We said yes, about twenty minutes before.

'You don't know where she went?' he asked.

'Yeah, I think she went to Drogheda,' one answered.

What the woman was wanted for wasn't really an issue to the drivers, as none of us ever thought to ask. It could have been anything. Times were hard and you lived by your wits. We didn't want our mate's trip to Tralee spoiled. He could get his money and make off into the sunset.

I remember another summer day during my run as a taxi driver when Evelyn and I were very short of money and still living on Kilfenora. It was hot and I decided to call it a day and go to the beach with Evelyn, the kids and my sister for the afternoon. We were getting ready when a woman came up to me and asked if my taxi was free. When I asked where she was going and she said Leixlip, I said it was certainly free. 'Sorry about that, Evelyn,' I said. Money was money and you had to take a good fare.

When the woman told me to pull over to a house in Kilfenora, I knew I shouldn't have got involved. The door opened and another woman threw a suitcase out into the front garden. There were clothes flying everywhere but my passenger gathered them up and piled them into the back of my taxi. A long-time Kilfenora neighbour, she was leaving her husband in my taxi and her husband's sister was at the door throwing her belongings out to her. Her husband was on the roof of a house further up the street, putting up a television aerial. His sister, who had just thrown the suitcases and clothes out in the garden, ran up the street to him, shouting, "Come down quickly, she's leavin' ya!'

Of course, I wanted my money but this scene was like the Keystone cops. Your man slid down the ladder as fast as he could, jumped into his buckety old Thames van and off with his friend in hot pursuit of my taxi. I delivered the woman safely to Leixlip, collected my fare and made my way back to Kilfenora to collect Evelyn and the others to go to the beach. I passed the Thames van on Conyngham Road on my way back to Kilfenora and waved, laughing and making rude gestures.

As I was contemplating what other job options might lie ahead, my brother-in-law, an architect named Christy Morris, and I were having regular discussions about the state of the Irish educational system; specifically, the attitudes of politicians and clergy toward the teaching of the Irish language. Christy and I regularly had lunch together at Kilfenora. Christy was married to my eldest sister, Ann, who had been so sharp and such a voracious reader as a child that our mother used to unscrew the light bulb from the lamp when she went to bed so she could be certain Ann didn't stay up all night with a book. Christy was a good match for Ann wits-wise and I loved him. I was about sixteen when Christy, six years my senior, met my sister and it was a great thing to have a smart, kind and lovely young man coming around to our house.

Christy was extremely gentle and gentlemanly and he managed to be a great organiser without having to resort to power plays. He proved that he could hold people's attention with his conviction when he founded the Language Freedom Movement (LFM), which I think of as the first civil rights group in Ireland. The thing that bothered Christy, me and the other LFM organisers most about the government's language policy as it was then, in the mid-1960s, was the underlying discrimination against those who couldn't speak Irish, or, as the LFM always pointedly referred to it, Gaelic. For the LFM, 'Irish' and 'Gaelic' were the same language but we preferred the term 'Gaelic' because we viewed it as the language of the past, not a modern language. At that time, students could pass their exams in Maths, English and all the other subjects but if they failed Irish they failed entirely. Postal workers who hadn't passed their Irish exams had to sign on in red ink in the morning, weren't allowed to own a duty and were not eligible for a pension, whereas the others signed on in blue ink, could own a duty and would receive a pension, all other things being equal. We felt that this was appalling if you take into account that the mother language in Ireland is English. The language of our ancestors was Gaelic. To us, it was just as logical to expect the people of Ireland to revert back to speaking Gaelic as it was to get the people of Peru speaking the language of the Incas.

What really seemed unreasonable to the founders of the LFM was Fianna Fáil's language policy at the time. Fianna Fáil was advocating unilingualism, not bilingualism, and the language it was pushing was Irish. For the country to have the gift of such an internationally useful language as English at its disposal and even to think about reverting to an ancient language that was barely, if at all, spoken outside Ireland, seemed totally illogical to the LFM. This wasn't to say that our group was advocating abolishing the teaching of Irish in schools; several of the founding members spoke Irish fluently and I had earned the gold Fáinne in the army, even if my motives in seeking the award had more to do with revenge than scholarship. The LFM wanted people to examine the true intentions behind the government's and the clergy's vehement support of Irish. Why was it so important to them to try to force – as we saw it, they were forcing – the country back into embracing Irish as its primary language?

The conclusions we arrived at, after numerous public meetings that could have easily passed for small riots in Dublin and further west, in Galway, were twofold. It came down to passionate ideology on the one hand and, as with so many other things, money on the other. We knew there were many Irish teachers, especially in the Christian Brothers, who were fanatical Gaeilgeoirí and whose mantra was to 'burn everything English but their coal'. They represented the absolute nationalists who hated England and everything England stood for, including the language. Then there was the fact that government grants were available in Gaeltacht areas purely *because* they were Gaeltacht areas, not on the basis of economic need, when there were areas in counties like Leitrim that were destitute but had no such grants available because the county was not Irish-speaking.

Christy, the rest of the LFM founders and I realised very early in the life of our group just how fanatical some of our opponents were. Christy remembers one of his favourites among the slogans of the opposition: 'Treason has no rights.' The membership of the LFM itself was varied. Christy wrote a letter to *The Irish Times* in 1966, announcing a gathering for interested parties in Buswell's Hotel, opposite the Dáil, and was astounded at the response. Many professors from different universities joined because they'd seen first-hand all the discrimination and politics involved in the teaching of Irish but hadn't yet got around to organising themselves to challenge it. There were students, bank managers, businessmen, architects and artists.

As soon as the LFM introduced itself to the public, the opposition organised itself in a flash, accusing us of being anti-Irish and anti-Ireland. We were called traitors and labelled 'West Brits', which I still laugh about today. The idea of someone born in Kimmage being a West Brit is so far removed from reality, it's just funny. There were a few members of the LFM who did possibly fit that description, like a good friend of mine from Foxrock, Finbarr Corry. Finbarr arrived at my house one day wearing a bowler hat and with a poppy pinned to his coat. My greeting included a warning that he'd be lucky if the neighbours on Kilfenora hadn't taken the wheels off his very swanky car by the time he left. But Finbarr was just as committed to the cause as any of the other LFM members, staying up nights to run flyers off on a copying machine and put up posters around the city. He even sat up in a car one night around Merrion Square, in stake-out mode, with a few others in the movement, to try to catch whoever was tearing down the 'Vote No to compulsory Irish' posters we had just put up. Other work for the LFM included driving up behind a bus, getting out at red lights and plastering LFM posters to the back of the bus before the light changed. Finbarr worked for Bank of Ireland and would sometimes be tempted to pull his jacket up over his face on these semi-covert escapades, lest he be seen by employers or colleagues. He could be fairly sure they would frown upon his involvement in such subversive activities.

The LFM's first public meeting after the initial gathering in Buswell's and a few smaller gatherings of the core group of founders was at the Mansion House in the spring of 1966. We had been having small meetings at a house in Mount Pleasant Place in Rathmines, which we used as our base of operations and for our correspondence. We soon realised that our post wasn't being delivered. Instructions to this effect had been left to the post office by someone who was obviously hostile to the movement's aims. We also knew we were being followed by Special Branch Gardaí who were monitoring our activities. I would become very familiar with the Special Branch in years to come, especially since one of the Gardaí most frequently assigned to follow me was a Kilfenora neighbour, Jackie Fagan, with whose brother I had been in Australia.

What with being followed and discovering the deliberate withholding of their post, LFM members knew that things were likely to get ugly at our first big public meeting. I had moved on to a job as a postman by this time and I was hearing things through the grapevine about the upcoming meeting – mainly that the LFM's critics were planning on breaking it up and causing trouble. When I reported this information back to the LFM committee, I realised my idea of what it meant to 'cause trouble' was totally different from that of my fellow founders. The committee envisaged a lot of people stamping their feet and rustling papers.

'You'll get your head kicked in maybe,' I said.

They did not believe it for a moment. I already knew where I fit into the group – among the LFM founders, I was the least genteel of all. The worst I've ever heard Christy Morris say in annoyance is, 'Oh, jingo mac.' Most of them had probably thrown very few digs in their lives. But however different they were from me, I admired them all and felt I had learned a lot from their example. Still, my admiration didn't change the fact that they were being naïve about the level of violence we could expect to see at our first big meeting.

On the night of the meeting, Dawson Street was jam-packed with people. Admission was free but the gates to the Mansion

House were locked before the meeting started. We were astounded that such a huge crowd had turned up. We had obviously hit a nerve. Layton Pratt, a young American PhD student at Trinity, wanted to create an LFM poster using the term 'sacred cow', but Christy Morris thought it was too incendiary. Layton argued that this just proved his point but Christy thought there was no value in giving the cows ammunition.

Father Ó Fiaich (later to become Cardinal) and another priest, two of the most outspoken members of the Dublin clergy and the staunchest advocates of the current language policy, were outside the gates at the front of the crowd, waiting for the meeting to start. In the spirit of good-natured debate and according to tacit gentlemanly rules, it was agreed that I should go out and invite them to come in ahead of the others so that they could take their seats and be nearer the speakers. I went out to them and extended the invitation and they flatly said no. As I turned to go back inside, someone from the crowd shouted that I was a 'quisling', a word meaning, roughly, 'traitor'. As they were opening the gates to let me back in, the two priests shouted, 'Rush the gates!' and the crowd started pouring in. I made a statement to the media later about what had happened and the two priests responded with solicitors' letters challenging me. I responded with a letter that said, in summary, 'See you in court', and heard nothing more about it.

There was a rush from the people inside the gates to keep them closed but I saw a young man with his head between the gate and the hinge, poised for serious injury, or worse, if the gates were to be shut again. The gates were opened and the crowd rushed in and I remember the LFM's opponents that night behaving in a totally despicable way, armed with Union Jacks and anti-LFM leaflets. We later described them in our LFM newsletter as demonstrating a 'frenzied, vocal solidarity', driven by an underlying 'crusading zeal'. Once they got inside, there was chaos. No one could be heard over the screaming and shouting. Christy

Morris, the chairman, could see within a second that there was no way this crowd would listen to the speeches we had planned, so he tried to tell everyone that the LFM panel would just take questions. But that turned out to be an impossibility too. When Christy looked out on the crowd, it reminded him of a large bar-room brawl more than anything else. Tomás Mac Giolla, a Sinn Féin leader, managed to get hold of the microphone and proclaim that Irish would be taught, if necessary, 'through the barrel of a gun.' I thought that the behaviour of Father Ó Fiaich, in particular, was appalling. He appeared to be acting no better than a drunken, obstreperous heckler. I used that exact phrase in a letter to The Irish Times later on. Whether he drank or not, I don't know, but those words described his behaviour. If I'd had the physical ability, I would have thrown him out.

My fellow LFM founder, Richard Clear, remembers the contradiction between the Christian values that Catholic priests were supposed to embody and the behaviour of the clergy that night: 'They were full of hate, not love,' he says. We could see that most of our critics didn't want to argue at all, they just wanted to attack. There were many among the LFM founders who were disappointed because they had actually thought that civilised debate about language policy was possible. The first Mansion House meeting put a cold stop to that idea. The meeting had deteriorated before it even began, morphing into riot and utter chaos. But with chaos comes publicity. And it got huge publicity.

As 1966 was the fiftieth anniversary of the Easter Rising and there were parades and celebrations all around Dublin, I suggested that the LFM participate in some of these in order to prove to the public that the group was just as Irish and as proud of Irish freedom as anybody else. The members agreed that this was a good idea and it was carried off successfully. Meanwhile, more branches of the LFM were sprouting up all over the country and we organised to send speakers to them from Dublin. It was an advantage if our speakers were fluent in Irish, to demonstrate, in as visible a way as possible, that it was not the language itself that the LFM was against. We had no trouble finding such speakers. One, Roddy Buckley, was set to speak in Galway, at the LFM's first meeting in the west, in the aftermath of the Mansion House meeting. Roddy was not just a fluent Irish speaker but a great public speaker all around. But as he and I approached the city, he discovered he didn't have his contact lenses with him, which was a big problem because he always used a script when he spoke. When we arrived at the venue, which had been switched from a hotel to a Church of Ireland hall because of the hotel's concerns about potential damages, there was another mob scene. I told the Gardaí I was trying to get in, to which a Garda replied dryly, 'Aren't we all.'

'No but we're the speakers,' I said.

The Gardaí made a path through the crowd and got us inside but it was just as packed as the Mansion House meeting and almost as rowdy. People were standing on the window sills outside, looking in. It didn't matter after all that Roddy had forgotten his contact lenses, because he wouldn't have been able to speak to the belligerent crowd. I took the microphone and announced that we would cut the speech we had planned and just do a questions-and-answers session, on condition that the crowd settled down and actually let the questions and answers be heard. There was still pushing and shoving, squirming and disruptions but unlike the Mansion House meeting, questions were actually asked and answered. A man in the audience even invited me to come on a holiday to the Gaeltacht free of charge. At the time I might have thought I was brave but I wasn't *that* fucking brave. I feared I would never get back from the Gaeltacht but it was very nice of him.

As the meeting wound down, I was tuned into the body language of the men in the front row and could see them trying to decide who would attack me and Roddy as soon as the meeting ended. I got the Gardaí to form a line at the front of the stage to create a barrier between me, Roddy and the crowd. We had been planning to spend the night in Galway and leave for Dublin in the morning but the Gardaí strongly suggested that it was in our best interest to leave right after the meeting. They offered to escort us out of town for about ten miles with a squad car.

Around the one-year anniversary of the first Mansion House meeting, in the spring of 1967, the LFM decided it was time for another meeting at the same venue, having taken on board the lessons learned from the first débâcle. It had become increasingly difficult to find venues to host our meetings. Our reputation preceded us and hotels and halls weren't willing to take the risk of having their rooms damaged by the whirlwind of violence that followed the LFM wherever it appeared. We had already been barred from a few places in Dublin, including Jury's Hotel.

Since I was the one who had most accurately predicted the level of violence at the first Mansion House meeting, the LFM decided I was their man to organise the security details for the second meeting, along with Michael Couth, another LFM member. Whereas admission to the first meeting had been free, we decided to charge seven shillings and sixpence for admission into this one. In other words, if you want to cause a riot, you pay the price. No one was allowed to sit in the front row, immediately in front of the panel of speakers. I arranged for one hundred stewards to be there and thirteen paid bouncers. The stewards were all volunteers from the LFM but the bouncers were hired for their size only, regardless of their personal politics. There was a strong Garda force keeping order outside and I had made arrangements with them that if someone was thrown out of meeting, the Gardaí would detain them for the length of it to stop further disruption.

Another thing that lent the second Mansion House greater gravity was its panel. The affable Gay Byrne, the most recognisable man in Ireland at the time as the host of the immensely popular

Late Late Show, had agreed not only to chair the meeting but to waive his fee. He said he would do it in the interest of free speech. I remember hearing that his wife, Kathleen Watkins, was sitting across the street in the Hibernian Hotel for the length of the meeting, biting her fingernails with worry that her husband would be torn to shreds. One of the panel members was writer John B. Keane. Keane had brought his own bodyguard along, a huge man. The increased security presence, both inside and outside the building, kept order and the meeting was able to go ahead without ending in a huge brawl, even though the place was packed to capacity.

The LFM's ultimate goal was to bring about a change in the government's language policy but realistically, its founders knew that these kinds of legal changes take years. Indeed, it was years before postal workers all signed on in the morning in the same colour ink, regardless of the level of proficiency they had displayed in their Irish exams. What the group really wanted was to get people talking and debating about language and all that it symbolised in Ireland. At a time when nearly everything to do with sex was still taboo, the LFM was the first movement to question what was really behind how Ireland expressed itself. The equal rights movements that challenged the limits of expression itself would follow soon after the LFM.

5

REFORM

While I was still working in the post office, a company called O'Donoghue leather merchants went into liquidation. This happened to be the company that made most of, if not all, the leather straps used to discipline children. O'Donoghue's had an auction to clear out the last of its stock and all the remaining leather straps, twenty-nine in all, went to one man who was the highest bidder, an architect named Martin Reynolds.

Martin Reynolds had been intensely interested in corporal punishment in schools for years. He had often written letters to the newspapers and articles in magazines about the brutality in Irish schools, injuries sustained by children and the powerlessness of parents under the system. Martin also made a habit of writing to the Christian Brothers and reform schools in a sort of one-man crusade against corporal punishment, which he wanted to see abolished in all Irish schools.

When Martin heard that O'Donoghue's was going out of business and having an auction, he saw his chance to create a moment of publicity for the cause and to invite others to join in it. He was a great source of information and afraid of no man. He seemed rather to enjoy confrontation, although in a refined, mostly genteel sort of way that, fittingly for a man fighting brutality, never involved physical violence. I'd known Martin for a while and had been working with him trying to restrain some of the most outrageous abuse in schools, so when he seized on O'Donoghue's closing as the moment to recruit others to the cause, I was there to help him to found Reform.

There was a lot of overlap between LFM and Reform members and the LFM veterans had learned that getting good publicity at the beginning of any campaign was vital. Everyone knew that if you wanted to shine the national spotlight on any topic, you had to get it on *The Late Late Show* with Gay Byrne, as it was the one television programme at the time that everyone was afraid to miss. Martin's purchase of the leather straps wasn't enough in itself to get airtime on the show. The bonfire that we decided to make with them at the Department of Education was.

The Saturday after the auction, our burgeoning group made arrangements with the press for journalists and photographers to show up at the Department of Education within five minutes of our scheduled protest so they'd be assured of good photographs but wouldn't draw so much attention that they'd be in danger of attracting the Gardaí. Someone had made a cardboard headstone with the lettering, 'The Death of Irish Education.' We also had a grill pan at the ready for the leather straps and people off to the side with fire extinguishers. The fire was lit and our protest march paraded from the Department of Education in Marlborough Street to O'Connell Street and back. In those days, this was more than enough to secure an invitation to *The Late Late Show*.

I was the representative from Reform who was chosen to appear on *The Late Late Show* panel the following week. It was my first television appearance and I was nervous. I was facing a few opponents who, at the time, had more experience than I did in front of cameras and talking to the media. One was Senator Seán Brosnan from the INTO (Irish National Teachers' Organisation), who denied that children were being beaten at all in schools and maintained that the public had reason only to praise Irish teachers. Another was Paddy Crosbie, a teacher at Brunswick Street CBS and the presenter of a children's radio programme called *The School Around the Corner*. Like Brosnan, Crosbie denied that children were being abused in schools. On the opposing side to Brosnan and Crosbie was a doctor, Cyril Daly, who regularly wrote letters to *The Irish Times* about the damaging effects of corporal punishment on children's physical and mental wellbeing.

When it was my turn to have a say, I felt it was my responsibility to tell the nation about the Irish Christian Brothers who had beaten me as a child and who I knew were still terrorising children. Paddy Crosbie and Senator Sean Brosnan railed against me, saying it was preposterous to claim the Christian Brothers were doing anything but good. I said they were disgraceful and I talked about some of the abuse I had seen first-hand through my work with Reform. Just before the music came up at the end of the show, I leaned forward to the camera and said, 'As I sit here tonight, the Irish Christian Brothers are abusing our children.' Seconds after the music began, an audience member – Gus Cribben, a man I had already encountered when he opposed the LFM – rushed up to take a swing at me. The day after the broadcast was a Sunday and people shouted after me in the street about biting the hand that fed me and that I should be ashamed of myself for saying such terrible things about the Brothers.

My father's relatives weren't impressed either. Two of my first cousins on the Crummey side were Christian Brothers themselves and the family idolised them. The rise of Reform marked the beginning of a period of alienation between me and members of my father's family that would worsen in years to come.

I think there's an important connection between the lack of unfair dismissal protection back then and how few people were willing to speak out against the Brothers and the Church. The Unfair Dismissals Act wasn't passed until 1977, so in 1967, when I was on *The Late Late Show*, social workers or others who wished to blow the whistle were immediately threatened with dismissal. I was fortunate that I was never too worried about unemployment. I was a postman when I was on *The Late Late Show* but I had already been an army gunner, bus driver, taxi driver, ice-cream man and underwear salesman. I knew I could find work of some kind to support my family if I were to be sacked from one job. In the variety of my work experience, I found great freedom.

I became a social worker for the ISPCC shortly after my appearance on *The Late Late Show*. I thought this would be an opportunity to crack down on some of the worst abuses in the schools but I was devastated to find that the ISPCC did not consider this area to be their remit. My superiors very quickly told me that my only concern was home visits. I couldn't see the logic in this, so we were at loggerheads from the beginning. In one case, I placed three children in care at Goldenbridge convent in an emergency on a Friday night. When I went back to collect them on Monday morning, I found that one of them had been beaten by a Sister. I told the nun I would break her neck if I had half a chance and, predictably, when I returned to my office a complaint had been made that I had used bad language. Which I had.

I was warned not to interfere in Goldenbridge again. But I told my case consultant that I saw my job as representing the underprivileged, vulnerable and downtrodden and that therefore I had every right – and responsibility – to interfere in Goldenbridge. I felt social workers shouldn't be seen, or think of themselves, as being paid by the establishment just to keep the pot from boiling over. But over time, I faced the terrible realisation that I was in a tiny minority that had this conviction.

We in Reform proved that we were media-savvy. There had also been a very public case of a teacher excessively beating a child in

1968, the year after our formation, that placed the issue squarely in the public domain, where it had never been before. David Moore was a child who had been beaten repeatedly both with a stick and a strap by a young Christian Brother, Joseph Quinn, at St Michael's National School in Inchicore. David's parents needed help badly and they contacted me through Reform.

Martin Reynolds and I and some others met David Moore and his parents and we found David to be a quiet, timid boy. His entire backside was severely bruised from the beatings he'd received from the Christian Brother. David's mother was devastated at what had been done to her child and she was more willing to challenge the school and the system than many other women in her position had been in the past. Martin and I interviewed several of David's classmates and found one boy, a neighbour of David's, who was willing to give evidence in court against Brother Quinn, with his mother's full support.

There was a firm of solicitors who I knew would take on cases that were edgy for their day, involving controversial social issues. The firm had a great respect for the idea of citizens' right to representation and it was a natural choice to represent the Moore family. The solicitors were briefed on the case and said they would take it. A summons for Brother Quinn was drawn up. No one knew what Brother Quinn's first name was, which was essential for the serving of the summons. When the school's office was called, they knew better than to give it out. So two of my physician friends, Jim Loughran and Paddy Randall, and I paid a visit to the school, cornered Brother Quinn against a wall at the end of the school day and told him that he could either give us his name or his head would go through the railings. He barked 'Joseph' and we served the summons on the spot.

There was much more work to be done in finding and preparing witnesses for the case. David had had a lay teacher at Goldenbridge convent, where he had been before St Michael's, whom he had loved and who the solicitors thought would make a good character witness. I went to the convent to serve her a summons but I knew the nuns would be expecting me, that it wouldn't be easy to get to her and that I'd better go with a few tricks up my sleeve. I brought someone with me, a much younger Kilfenora man named Teddy Mulvaney, to wait outside and watch the gates with the instruction that he should follow the first woman who wasn't in a habit. I went into the convent and was told by one nun, who was kindly enough, that I'd have to see the principal of the school, Sister Anne, who in turn told me politely that the teacher I was looking for was not on the premises.

I told her that was a shame but that I had a summons for a sister who *was* on the premises. I served it to the nun who had first greeted me, who was now standing next to Sister Anne. By now, I'd learned that it always paid to do my homework. I had found out the name of one of the other nuns who I knew was teaching there but who had no connection to the David Moore case and I was using her as a bluff in order to get the sisters to agree to tell me where David's teacher was.

They nearly fainted, the two of them. The nun I had served the summons to said that they never went as witnesses, even if the place was burgled or broken into, out of the court's consideration for them. I felt that 'consideration' didn't figure in this situation. A boy had been badly beaten and if there was a teacher at a convent who could help his case by testifying, I wanted to do my best to see that she testified.

Sister Anne asked me to excuse her for a few minutes and I knew she was calling her solicitor. When she came back, oddly, the first thing she said to me was, 'Mr Crummey, would you like to smoke?' I thanked her but told her I didn't smoke. She asked me if I would take the summons back from the nun I'd just served it on if she told me where the lay teacher I'd wanted to see in the first place was. I said of course I would and she gave me an address in Tyrconnell Road where I could find her.

When I went there, I found Teddy Mulvaney at the gate hanging around, wondering what to do. As soon as he had seen the lay-teacher emerge from the school, he had, as instructed, followed her to her house. But in the pre-mobile-phone era, he didn't really know what to do after that, as he had no way of letting me know where he was. When I went in to speak to the teacher, I found her courteous and charming and she said that David Moore had been a pleasure to teach: he was a lovely little boy and she couldn't imagine him causing any trouble. I served her summons and was delighted with myself.

Just a few days later, on a Friday afternoon, the woman who had agreed to have her son give evidence in David Moore's favour rang me and Martin Reynolds in distress. She said two Christian Brothers from St Michael's had been to her house to tell her that they would be taking her son to their own solicitor the next morning to make a statement. There had been no asking in question. She said she had told them her son was giving evidence for David and that she didn't want him to go with them but they had said she didn't have a choice and that they'd be at her house at 8:30 in the morning. I told her Martin and I would be at her house the next morning at 7:30.

Promptly at 8:30, a car pulled up to the house and the two Christian Brothers got out. The woman met them at the door and told them she didn't want her son to go with them. They pushed past her into the house without answering.

Martin and I were there and we were ready. 'Out, fucking now,' we said, standing up from our seats in the parlour.

The Brothers were startled but, glaring at us, went off in a huff without much of a scene. The last thing they'd been expecting to see at the house were two threatening (if physically unassuming) men barring their path. When the trial began shortly after, the solicitors' senior counsel interviewed the lay teacher – the woman I'd worked so hard to get a summons to before the trial – but found her unsuitable to testify. I can only assume the nuns intimidated her into silence. The testimony from the other witnesses, combined with the horrific photographs of David's injuries, were enough to convince the jury that he had received excessive beatings from Brother Joseph Quinn and he was awarded one shilling in contemptuous damages. The citizens on the jury couldn't deny the abuse had happened in the face of such solid facts and evidence but they still couldn't bring themselves to make the Christian Brothers pay, or to admit that the victim deserved compensation. Shocking as it seems today, the difficulties and resistance we encountered as we were building David's case indicated that even a guilty verdict was unlikely, in spite of the strength of the evidence. Neither Martin Reynolds nor I, nor anyone from the solicitors, had been able to find an Irish doctor to testify on David Moore's behalf to the extent of his injuries. We had to get a foreign doctor to fulfil that role.

The media attention the Moore case attracted wasn't confined to Ireland. The National Broadcasting Corporation (NBC), then one of only three major television networks in the United States, sent a film crew to Ireland in the immediate aftermath of the case to make a documentary about the Irish education system. The use of corporal punishment featured heavily in the film. It even included a segment where Gus Cribben, the man who attacked me after my *The Late Late Show* appearance, demonstrated his caning techniques. Cribben later told RTÉ that he'd been misled as to the purpose of the documentary. At least one other teacher who had admitted on tape that he used corporal punishment also claimed he'd been similarly tricked. The film was shown in the US to the shock and embarrassment of Irish officials, teachers and, of course, the Christian Brothers.

Shortly after the trial, the Moore family emigrated to Canada. The first family in the country's history ever to bring a case against the Christian Brothers found it too difficult to live in Ireland and send their children to school amid such attention. With Reform's appearance on *The Late Late Show* and all the print coverage the group received, parents were beginning to realise there were people they could contact if they felt their child had been mistreated by a teacher. Before Reform, they had to deal with abuse by themselves, if at all. Often, they didn't get past the principal of the school in question. I had never told my own mother about the beatings I'd endured at the hands of the Christian Brothers because I knew how upset and also how powerless she would be to do anything to change the situation. But schools feared bad publicity more than almost anything and the media turned out to be one of Reform's best allies.

Word quickly got out around the schools of Dublin that there was a new action group taking on teachers on behalf of parents whose children had been abused in the classroom. There was one school on the northside of Dublin where a child was being beaten repeatedly. The child's parents had been to the principal and were treated with the usual contempt. The parents contacted the secretary of Reform, Maura Carthy, to see if there was anything the group could do to help them.

Martin Reynolds and I and two other members of Reform talked to the parents and the child and we asked the child to explain exactly where the principal's office was in the building so we could walk in without having to ask for directions. The four of us walked into the school and went straight to the principal's office. We shut the door behind us. One of the men sat on the principal's desk, intentionally displaying lack of respect and aggression. The principal had completely supported the teacher who had beaten the child and for a few brief moments he stood firm. The first thing he did was to threaten to phone the Gardaí. We said we would also ring the press so that they could come to the school and take photographs of everyone, including the principal. We gave him the ultimatum: either talk there and then or have the media's magnifying lens fixed on his own house and feel the burn. We made it abundantly clear that a Garda presence was the least of our worries.

The principal backed down. It seemed the only thing people like him understood was intimidation. Here was a situation where the principal had defended a teacher knowing the extent of the abuse that had taken place, closing ranks immediately and bullying any parents who dared to challenge him. But faced with the threat of public exposure, the ranks began to open as those in charge feared for their own standing.

We told the principal that the parents were on standby and expecting a cringing apology both from himself and from the teacher. We promised him that if the teachers touched the child again, the press really would be delivered to his doorstep. The teacher was called to the office and the principal ripped him apart in front of me and the others. Then the parents were summoned and the teacher delivered the promised apology, under duress. But the only thing the principal ripped him apart for was that he had brought us down on his school: it wasn't because he had beaten the child. It didn't matter who was right or wrong: the principal just wanted the easiest way out.

Similar scenes were enacted all over Dublin and the surrounding areas, with similar results.

At this point I should make clear I don't oppose a loving mother or father spanking a child. When my daughter Elizabeth annoyed me one day to the point that I was running up the stairs after her, she pivoted around to face me and said, 'Reform, how are you?'

I wasn't surprised and, in spite of myself, felt a twinge of pride in my eldest child.

6

Sex Comes to Ireland

It was the late 1960s and I was getting tired of postal work. Occasionally, I was able to cause a respectable amount of aggro. There was the day when I was collecting post from the pillar boxes at the GPO and I was overcome by the urge to fit myself inside the box so that I could see out through the slot. I reached my hand out to grab a letter from a lady's fingers, causing uproar and getting myself booted out of the building and back to Sheriff Street, where I was based that day. Then there was the case of Máirtín Ó Caidhn, the Trinity College Irish professor who was vehemently opposed to the LFM and found out it was I who was delivering his post. He told me that if he saw me near his postbox again he'd deck me, so other arrangements had to be made.

There was also a night I was asked, as was the custom, to consult a list of street names and put all the post for them aside for the Special Branch officers to examine later. I never complied with such requests anyway, just left out advertisements and bills instead of real correspondence, but this night I got a shock when I saw the list. There was Kilfenora, my own street. I was fairly sure the Special Branch wouldn't have had much reason to want to see the post of any of my neighbours!

Even though I wasn't getting any great fulfilment from my job at the post office, I wasn't yet sure what was next for me. I lived for my night-time meetings and rallies, where the average man's typical night probably started and ended with a few pints at the pub with friends. I much preferred putting myself in front of a hostile crowd to talk about language policy or to serve a summons. For my friends and me, these were serious issues. But they were also exciting and, in a way, a form of entertainment. Beside all that, the pub wasn't as natural a habitat for me as it was for most Irishmen. I was in my late thirties before I ever raised a glass of alcohol to my lips.

As Reform gained a reputation for itself as a group that got results, Maura Carthy, the secretary, was receiving more and more phone calls from parents. Reform's own members were observing a huge amount of abuse, of which the doctors among us were especially aware. One Reform member, Doctor Jim Loughran, was particularly affected by a case of abuse he saw in Skerries, where he had his practice. A little girl had been injured by a lay teacher in class and her father brought her to see Doctor Loughran, who reported the case back to Reform. The group did their standard investigation and found what should have been a clear-cut case for damages against the school and the teacher for the injuries the girl had sustained. But the girl's father was a self-employed mechanic who had a large family of ten children and the local priest had paid him a visit to say that if he proceeded against the school, not another car would pass his garage door. The father dropped the whole matter.

This particular case made it very clear to Reform members that parents who had very large families to look after were vulnerable in many ways when it came to standing up for their rights, especially against the schools. Jim Loughran, from his experience in general practice and as a member of Reform, knew that it was time to do something to help couples to plan their families so that they could choose how many children they had. Doctor Loughran recruited some colleagues and friends, formed a committee and set up a company called the Fertility Guidance Company Limited. Our opening night was in a clinic at Number 10 Merrion Square. I was a company member and Evelyn and I were both there for the big event.

The laws in Ireland in the late 1960s were designed to make it exceedingly difficult for women to have access to contraception. It was illegal both to sell and to advertise contraceptive devices, with the exception of the birth control pill, which women could get with a doctor's prescription but only under the guise of its use as a 'cycle regulator'. It was also illegal to import contraceptive devices but, importantly, it was not illegal to use contraceptives once they were inside the country.

The Catholic Church couldn't have been clearer about its disapproval of any use of contraception as a sinful action in itself. Millions of Irish women and men believed that it was a sin to have sex before marriage and they were also convinced that if they did have premarital sex, it was a double sin to use contraceptives. Many women who had the money and the knowledge took the train to Belfast, where condoms, jellies and other devices were available in chemists' shops and could easily be smuggled back in through customs. Others ordered similar devices through the post from England and they were shipped into Ireland in plain, inconspicuous packaging. But there were thousands of women who were either too poor or too unaware to do these things and they were the ones who were saddled with children they hadn't planned for and couldn't afford.

There was great trepidation and a barely containable anxiety on the opening night of the clinic in Merrion Square. If fights had broken out over the country's language policy, what would the reaction be to a topic that revolved around sex? I couldn't imagine not being involved in the clinic's opening. Syl Collins had remarked that I was selling knickers on the street in Ireland before it was even acceptable to say the word 'knickers'. I had grown up on a street full of houses that had been bursting with children, sometimes half a dozen or more to a single bedroom, and I had seen first-hand the strain it put on families, both financial and emotional. The directors of the Fertility Guidance Company had agreed that I would be the one to supply the clinic's first two patients on its opening night. I decided that there was no reason to look too far from home for our first patient, so I nominated Evelyn to go in to Doctor Loughran for advice on contraception.

The second patient's circumstances were different. Since the name of the clinic was, for obvious political reasons, the 'Fertility' Guidance Company instead of the 'Family Planning' Guidance Company, we knew it would be best if one of our first two patients was actually seen to have a fertility problem with which she needed guidance. I had a friend, a young woman who had been married for some time and had no children, but was anxious to start a family. She went in to see Doctor Loughran and he asked her a few basic, gentle questions about herself, her husband and their life together. One of the things she mentioned was that her father-in-law was sleeping in the bedroom next to theirs. Doctor Loughran's best medical advice was for the woman to move the grandfather to the room over the garage. She took his advice and conceived almost immediately.

The doctors at the clinic, with Jim Loughran at the helm, were able to write prescriptions for the pill but they still had the problem of importing all the other contraceptive devices they needed. Creams, gels and condoms were easy enough to get from England in the post or to bring back on the train from Belfast but they also needed slightly bulkier items like diaphragms and coils, which clinic patients had to order from the Family Planning Association in England. They would come through customs labelled as 'toilet requisites.' Whenever any of the members of the Fertility Guidance Company went to England for any reason, they tried to get as many different contraceptives back through customs as they could. One woman's suitcase was opened to reveal scads of diaphragms that she had taken out of their packages. When the young customs official asked what they were, she replied, 'Jam pot covers,' and he waved her through. Being a good Catholic lad, he had no idea what he was looking at.

The clinic had no trouble filling its appointment book but the members of the Fertility Guidance Company were on completely new ground and problems cropped up for which we had to find creative solutions. For instance, a postal strike meant that all the women who had been ordering the creams and gels that went with their diaphragms had to get them elsewhere or find something else that would work. One of the committee members, a gynaecologist, asked a pharmacist friend if there was something else that would suit while the strike was on and he said that Macleans toothpaste would do the trick. A woman at the meeting quipped that she had hoped it would be Colgate, so that they could be assured of the 'ring of confidence' (the company's slogan) in a different sense from its original meaning.

There were other big decisions for the company and the committee to make. We weren't afraid to push the law to its limit. Jim Loughran was especially keen to see how far the clinic could go before the Gardaí would come knocking. When the clinic first opened, the patients themselves were responsible for ordering their own diaphragms and gels from England once the doctor had determined their size. But Doctor Loughran wanted to see if the clinic could start ordering the supplies directly and passing them on to patients: would the authorities come after us then, when we were clearly importing contraceptives for distribution? The legislation outlawing contraceptives in the Republic of Ireland dated back to the 1935 Criminal Law Amendment Act, which read: 'It shall not be lawful for any person to sell, or expose, offer, advertise, or keep for sale or to import or attempt to import into Saorstát Éireann for sale any contraceptive.'

The emphasis of the law appeared to be on the *sale* of contraceptives and the clinic never charged for them, instead accepting voluntary 'donations' in exchange. The Merrion Square clinic began directly importing diaphragms and distributing them to patients. Articles about contraception were splashed across the women's pages of the three major newspapers, *The Irish Times*, the *Irish Press* and the *Irish Independent*, which, with the burgeoning women's liberation movement, often covered the most controversial topics. The messages from the pulpit became even more forceful because of all the attention: contraception was a sin and good Catholics shouldn't even consider using it. It was a fabulously exciting time and my friends and I in the family planning movement couldn't wait to see what would happen next.

Other groups soon splintered off from the Fertility Guidance Company, headed by founders of the original group. Within a few years of the opening of the Merrion Square clinic, Doctor Loughran and others boldly decided to change the company's name to the 'Irish Family Planning Association' (IFPA). They opened a new clinic under the IFPA's name in Mountjoy Square. A Fertility Guidance Company founder, Robin Cochran, and I, set up another clinic under the name 'Family Planning Services' in Pembroke Road and decided to distribute condoms and other contraceptives as blatantly as possible to see, yet again, how far we could push the laws. When Anne Connolly set up the Well Woman Clinic, I saw this as complementary to our clinic, not a competitor. That way, if one clinic was shut down, people would still have somewhere else they could go for their medical advice and contraceptives.

With the help of my family, I filled orders for contraceptives from my own house. Like well-trained operatives on an assembly line, Evelyn and I and our four daughters, Elizabeth, Deirdre, Edel and Jane, had a regular post-Mass ritual on Sundays of answering letters from women in response to ads I had personally placed in *Women's Way* magazine advertising free condoms. I knew it was inevitable that someone would try to shut down my one-man (or, more accurately, one-family) operation but I was flooded with requests from women who needed contraceptives, some desperately, and the most important thing for the time being was getting them out in the post.

I had a personal arrangement with London Rubber, then one of the biggest producers of condoms, whereby the company was donating large numbers of condoms to the cause of Irish family planning. I had them shipped from London over to Portadown in Northern Ireland and every second Saturday I'd drive up to collect them and smuggle them across the border. Occasionally, I was stopped at customs checkpoints but at that time the authorities had much more serious concerns on their radar to do with violent IRA activity. Large quantities of condoms were the least of their worries. There was one occasion on which I was in a long queue of cars at the border waiting to be checked at customs when I realised customs were stopping only every third car and waving the ones in between through. I counted back and saw I would be stopped, so I jumped out of my car and opened the bonnet, feigning engine trouble, until I had waved the car behind me ahead and rearranged the queue.

Saturday was collection day and Sunday was my family's distribution day. I found some of the letters responding to my advertising free condoms heartbreaking. The tragedy of these letters at that time was that the women writing them felt that I was sitting in judgement on them so they had to convince me that they had a drunken husband who wouldn't take no for an answer. Or that they'd already had three children and one handicapped child…and so on. I found this terribly sad, when it was their basic right to have them if they wanted them.

Evelyn would answer the letters as she had better handwriting and spelling than me. Elizabeth, our eldest daughter, who was about fourteen at the time, was in charge of placing the condoms in the envelopes. Deirdre, about a year younger than Elizabeth, did the same for the creams and gels. Edel, next in the queue, was on diaphragm duty and Jane, the baby, who was too young to be

My father, Sergeant Frank Crummey (far left),
with his Garda colleagues in Louisburg, County Mayo, c. 1930.

My father on the slopes of Croagh Patrick,
County Mayo, after burying his first child.

On my First Holy Communion day, 1943,
with my godmother, 'Chick' Greene.

My Confirmation class in Crumlin CBS, 1947.
I am in the second row, fifth from the left (above the '19' of '1947').

The only surviving photo of the entire Crummy family. From left: Anne, my father,
me, my mother, my twin Sadie and Marie.

My departure for Australia, 1956. Seeing me off at Dún Laoghaire were: front row, from left: Harry Eastman, Noel Kenny, Frank Ogilsby, Eddie Cummins, Jim Farrell, Paddy Lane, Frank Kenny. Middle row, from left: Mrs Gleeson, Mrs Fagan, Declan Walsh, Maura Fagan, Frank Davis, Raymond Burke, Evelyn Ormsby (my future wife), Paddy McPartland, Ena McPartland, Sadie Crummey (my twin sister), Eileen Shortall, Marie Crummey (my sister), Beatrice Burke, Mr Fagan. Back row, from left: Mr Cullen, Mrs Cullen, Denis Finn, Pat Fagan, Jim Kenny, Pat Cullen, myself, Ann Shortall, Malachy Burke, Dessie Lane and Benny Kenny.

From left: myself, Noel Kenny and Harry Eastman leaving Dún Laoghaire for Australia, 1956.

Myself with (from left) Pat Cullen, Evelyn Ormsby and Anne and Eileen Shortall on the day I left for Australia, 1956.

Ronnie Delaney arriving in Melbourne for the 1956 Olympic Games (my photograph).

From left: Declan Walsh, Mary Roberts, my cousin, my aunt Kitty and I, the day after Declan and I were arrested in Belfast in 1957.

Evelyn and I on our wedding day, 4 April 1961

Dessie Noone and I on the day we joined London Transport.

Clarence Best, my conductor with London Transport.

My family, 1972. From left: Evelyn with baby Frank, Edel, Elizabeth, Deirdre, Jane and I.

The launch of Reform, 1967. From left: Senator Owen Sheehy-Skeffington, myself, Proinsias Mac Aonghusa and Richard Clear.

The Late Late Show *panel discusses corporal punishment, 1967. From left: Paddy Crosbie, myself and Dr Cyril Daly.*

in charge of anything, tore the used stamps off the envelopes to bring them into the nuns in support of the foreign missions. Little did the nuns know what these letters were about. If they had, they wouldn't have taken them.

My family and I were still living in my beloved Kilfenora home with my mother and it couldn't have been much of a shock to the old neighbours that the boy they had called 'Little Mouth' had grown up to be an even bigger mouth. Some of them saw me as entirely outrageous but I was born and raised on the street and was therefore one of their own. Even if they thought it was scandalous that the Crummey family's Sunday activity was packaging and posting condoms, when it came right down to it, I was still all right. I had a sixteen-millimetre educational film about family planning and contraception that I would often have to rewind in the house so it would be ready for its next audience. My children could probably have recited it from memory from seeing it so many times. People would have thought from the way I was rearing my children that they would have grown up absolutely promiscuous and wild but they grew up lovely and gentle and fairly conservative and they made up their own minds. I remember inviting Elizabeth out on a protest once and her declining because she didn't 'approve' of my friends (her words) but young Frank accompanied me on demonstrations many times.

In the 1970s, the journalist Peigín Doyle wrote an article about me in *The Irish People* that started with the sentence, 'There are probably people in this country who have nightmares about Frank Crummey.' She continued: 'Which is rather funny when you realise that probably most of them have never even heard of the name but when you are someone who wants to see contraception legalised, you have a capacity to raise unquiet dreams.' The article pointed out the contradiction between the perception many people would have had of me as a seedy, childless man carelessly handing out condoms and the person I really was

– an unorthodox, cheerful father of five (our youngest, Frank, was born in 1972). Peigín described me as having an 'impish sense of fun,' and appearing 'slight, wiry and overworked'.

I'm sure some people have wondered why a happily married father of five was so passionate about making contraceptives easily available to Irishwomen. I witnessed the difficulties and desperation of hundreds of families with many more hundreds of children on Kilfenora throughout my childhood. I love children and would like all children to be truly wanted, instead of being looked on as additional mouths to feed in a family. It has always made sense to me that giving adults the power to choose exactly how many children they would like to have and when is the best way to make that happen.

I've heard it said that many men regret not spending more time with their children but I spent plenty of time with mine when they were growing up. The most important things you can give your children are memories. All my children believed, for far too long, that the Wellington Monument in the Phoenix Park was filled with sweets and that on one day a year the bronze panels at the base were ceremoniously opened to spill them out for children to collect. Sometimes I'd come home with sweets in my pockets and tell them what a beautiful sight it was and what a shame they had missed it.

My children knew that if Evelyn was ever away or having another baby in hospital and I was in charge, they were in for a few days of wonderful treats. I would let them sleep all around the floor in my bedroom and tell them funny, silly stories late into the night. One of them, who shall remain nameless, would get so excited and laugh so hard she would wet herself. Late at night another would ask the time-honoured questions that are rites of passage for parents – like the ever-popular 'How are babies made?' Even though I was accustomed to speaking to hostile crowds on reproduction and contraception, I suddenly found myself struggling and stammering in the dark with my own small children, searching for the gentlest and easiest combination of words to help them to understand.

Much as they loved their father, being a Crummey child had its own unique challenges. Jane, at six years old and spectacularly small for her age, opened her schoolbag one day to find not her sandwiches but a pelvic model and various contraceptives, including tubes of the usual creams and gels. She had accidentally switched bags with me in the car that morning. She was in tears because she was without her lunch but the nuns were in an absolute uproar. It hadn't escaped my notice that whenever I appeared in the schoolyard, all the nuns seemed to vanish as if by a magic spell. One day a brave young lay teacher approached me and asked if I was Frank Crummey. When I said I was, she said, 'I expected you to have cloven feet and at least two small horns,' smiled and walked away.

The women's pages of the newspapers were pushing the contraception issue into the public consciousness and, judging by newspaper sales and the buzz about the articles, it was the most controversial topic of its time. But the people running the Fertility Guidance and Family Planning associations knew we had to reach people on a more personal level than by mass-circulated newsprint. Messengers were sent out on educational missions all over the country, to talk about contraceptive methods and choices.

I loved going around and speaking, mostly to ladies' clubs and other women's groups, like local branches of the Irish Countrywomen's Association. I always took my bag of visual aids (the same bag that had traumatised Jane and the nuns) and various charts and diagrams to make it easier for audiences to understand things they might not have ever even heard of before, let alone laid eyes upon. My bag always included a plastic pelvic model with movable parts, condoms, creams, gels, IUDs and diaphragms. My usual partner in crime was Pat O'Donovan, a housewife with a lovely, cultured accent and a fine ladylike way about her. I knew it was smart to have both a man and a woman giving talks so that if any of the women in the audience had questions afterwards, they would have their choice of who they felt more comfortable asking. It also helped that Pat was married with children of her own and therefore had more credibility with audiences than a young, single woman might have had.

There was always someone, in every audience we spoke to, no matter how liberal an area it was, who was totally opposed to us and our ideas and viewed us as sinful. There was the night in Dublin when everything seemed to be going smoothly, with good audience participation, until suddenly there was a dead silence in the crowd. I looked around to see that the local priest had entered at the back of the room. I realised that there was no way the talk could continue to be as relaxed as it had been and there was no sense in ignoring the priest's presence. So I invited him up to the panel so that if he had something to say, he could be heard and included.

Sometimes you could feel the hostility in the air, where there had been a row on the committee about inviting us in the first place. There were always people totally opposed to you, people who totally supported you and a few with genuinely open minds, who had come to listen to you. Obviously that was the section you aimed at. Although we were a good deal in demand in the year or so after the first clinics began popping up in Dublin, there was no request Pat and I would turn down. We arrived in Letterkenny one night to speak to a crowd of forty or fifty people, the average age of whom looked to be about sixty-five. At least three of them were on Zimmer frames. I turned around and said, 'For Jesus sake, Pat, how am I going to give this crowd a talk?' Instead of my usual speech, I sat up on the table in the front of the room and told the funniest stories I could think of about family planning in Ireland and the history of family planning in England. At the end of the night, one of the ladies shuffled up to me on her Zimmer frame and told me that she was far beyond being concerned about methods of contraception herself but she had never laughed so much. She handed me twenty pounds and told me to use it for some women who couldn't afford contraceptives.

Pat and anyone else I ever travelled around with to give talks thoroughly enjoyed themselves on our treks across the country. We were experienced enough at thinking on our feet to avoid most total disasters. But there was always room for improvement in our talks and Pat and I knew each other well enough to be brutally honest with each other about them.

The debate over contraceptives expanded in the newspapers, on television, at the women's clubs all over the country and, finally, in the courts. The McGee case in 1973 involved a married woman with a medical intolerance to the pill who argued that she should be allowed to use contraceptives legally in the Republic of Ireland. The judge ruled that denying Mrs McGee the use of contraceptives was a violation of her bodily integrity and allowed that private citizens could now legally import contraceptives into Ireland for their own personal use. Importation for distribution and sale was still forbidden but we family planning advocates were still pleased with the ruling – it allowed a bit of a loophole.

On one of my runs up to the North and back following the McGee ruling, I was stopped coming through Balbriggan by Gardaí doing an arms check with 40,000 condoms in the boot of my car. The McGee case allowed me to tell the Gardaí I was importing them for my own personal use, believing I might have a legal leg to stand on. I was lucky that day. The sight of a small, wiry man insisting that the massive shipment of condoms was just for him, and that he would challenge them under EEC law if they booked him, appealed to the sense of humour of the Gardaí. The things they were looking for were made of steel, not rubber. 'Ah, go way,' they finally told me. I like to think I gave them a great story to tell.

There were more public debates and rallies and they were always packed. From the late 1960s, when the first controversial articles appeared in the then brand-new women's page of *The Irish Times* and, shortly afterwards, the women's pages of the other two national newspapers, the *Irish Press* and the *Irish Independent*, contraception was one of the hottest issues for nearly a decade. I liked to be one of the people in the spotlight, or at least to make sure that someone else who was well-informed was representing our side.

Irishwomen United, a radical feminist group calling for free legal contraception for all Irish women, organised a rally at Liberty Hall in November 1975 that drew a huge crowd. Mary Robinson and I, and one of my staunchest opponents in the Catholic Church, Father Denis Faul, were among the speakers. Mary Robinson, then a Senator, had been trying to get a bill passed in the Oireachtas for the previous several years that would legalise contraception for 'bona fide' (married) couples. The bill wasn't progressive enough for Irishwomen United, not least because it didn't provide for government funding of contraceptives; nor was it satisfactory to me, because it still restricted the legal use of contraceptives to married couples.

Father Denis Faul, a devoted man of the cloth, branded Robinson's proposed bill the beginning of the ruin of Irish society. He claimed that 'adultery and abortion would be on the rates', if Robinson's bill were passed, and that contraceptives helped to spread venereal diseases and sexual perversion to the married state. None of these arguments were new to me; they were the Church's standard reaction to the idea of contraception.

'I don't see how Catholics can achieve salvation if they never have the opportunity to avoid temptation,' I said in response to Father Faul's speech. 'I am damned if I am going to allow the Catholic Church to impose its rules on me,' I continued. 'We have no monopoly on morality. We have a deplorable social state with problems like alcoholism and broken marriages.'

There was another debate in Galway that Evelyn went along to, sitting in the audience as I spoke. I looked out from the podium and recognised the woman sitting next to Evelyn. She had written scads of letters to the paper opposing everything I advocated. 'He should be castrated,' she said passionately to Evelyn during the course of my speech. Evelyn nodded and smiled politely.

I appeared at these debates, slight and small, pointing out again and again that the emperor really wasn't wearing any clothes. If many Irish people still thought that following the Church's rules, restrictions and teachings would protect them from the scourges of vice and sin, I wanted to make sure they knew there was no such guarantee – in fact, quite the opposite. The Church's denial that sex is an enormous part of human relationships and its unwavering doctrine forbidding any sexual act outside of marriage was, in my eyes, enormously damaging to the health and wellbeing of all Irish people, not least Catholic priests. For me, the clerical sexual abuse scandals that emerged in the 1990s and the revelations that some of the country's most prominent clerics had had covert relationships with women and even fathered children, were the most concrete proof of that damage.

As the 1970s wore on, I continued my work with Family Planning Services even as I changed jobs time and again. One day in 1977, when I was working for myself as a private investigator, I was driving through Finglas and the driver behind me kept flashing his lights. I thought I must have had a flat tire, so I pulled over. The car pulled in behind me and a journalist got out. He asked me if I was aware that a booklet on family planning that the Irish Family Planning Association had put together and was distributing had been banned by the censorship board.

'Don't be silly,' I said.

'No, I'm telling you,' the journalist said. 'It was published today in the *Iris Oifigiúil*.'

I was familiar with the *Iris* – it was an official government publication that listed, among other things, banned books. If you made it into that, you were made. This was interesting news. I asked the journalist if he knew on what grounds it had been banned and he replied that it was labelled 'indecent and obscene'.

The booklet was entitled, *Family Planning: A Guide for Parents and Prospective Parents*. It was sixteen pages long, including the table of contents. The cover photograph, in technicolour green and black, showed a smiling family of four – an attractive couple with a young boy and girl, all holding hands, facing the camera on what was probably meant to look like their weekly post-Mass walk in the park. Far from containing any prurient material or even the somewhat crudely hand-drawn diagrams of the male and female reproductive systems that were becoming standard in educational pamphlets of this type, the booklet in its original form contained nothing but text. Later on it was amended and reprinted to include basic drawings, when patients reported that they had trouble following the text without illustrations.

There were two main sections, the first titled 'Effective Family Planning Methods,' which included the pill, the intra-uterine device, the diaphragm and sterilisation. The other section, 'Less Effective Family Planning Methods,' included the rhythm method, the condom, foams and jellies, withdrawal and complete abstinence. The last two pages consisted of names and addresses of organisations and clinics, where parents and prospective parents could go for advice and medical appointments. The first two names on the list were the IFPA's own clinics, in Synge Street and Mountjoy Square, but the next two were the Catholic Marriage Advisory Council and the Church of Ireland Marriage Counselling Service.

'If you have found this booklet helpful, please pass it on to a friend,' the last line read.

Even though it was sort of a badge of honour that the book was banned, the fact that it was banned on the grounds of being 'indecent and obscene' was deeply frightening to me. The booklet had been put together by three medical members of the IFPA committee: Jim Loughran, David Nowlan and Robert Towers. It was purely, unquestionably educational in nature.

When the journalist asked me for a quote on the side of the road in Finglas that day, after delivering the censorship news, I said impulsively, 'I'll sue the bastards.'

There was great publicity the next day, as I knew there would be. The directors of Family Planning Services got together and decided the best thing to do would be to enjoy the great wave of free public exposure. We agreed to organise a meeting that was half-press conference, half-protest at our office in Pembroke Road the next afternoon at 2:30. At this meeting we'd distribute – illegally – the booklet. I rang Donnybrook Garda Station to invite the Gardaí along to do their duty and arrest us for circulating banned literature. In the meantime, I'd been on to my solicitors and asked them to issue proceedings against the Censorship Board and the Attorney General.

The next day, when we were getting ready for the press conference and we'd made the arrangements for RTÉ to come out and film it, we realised we only had three copies of the book. And then I realised I hadn't got a crowd to buy the book either. I knew who to call. I rang Gaj's restaurant.

'Margaret, I need a crowd at half-past two,' I said to Margaret Gaj. I told her what it was for.

'Leave it with me,' she said.

At 2:30 on the dot, cars began pulling up and some of my regular lunchtime companions from Gaj's appeared. Among the group who came to purchase this book was Lady Christine Longford, who was about eighty years of age at the time. It was a very successful press conference: we suggested that RTÉ set up their cameras in a strategic way so that it wasn't obvious that the same three books were coming back in and going out again to the next 'customer.'

The Gardaí didn't show up until the cameras were gone and most of the excitement was finished. An inspector and sergeant came inside to speak to me.

'Mr Crummey,' the inspector asked, 'did you break the law?'

'I did, indeed,' I said cheerily. I picked up one of the three booklets, handed it to the inspector and said, 'You can have that.'

The inspector took the book, leafed through it and said nothing, his eyes fixed on the text.

'Ahem,' I said.

The inspector looked up.

'By the way,' I said, 'I've just broken the law again. I've distributed a banned book to you.'

The inspector continued flipping through the booklet and finally said, 'Can I keep it for the wife?'

I was true to my word, or, rather, my comment to the reporter in Finglas. In the case that became Crummey v Ireland, I sued both the Censorship Board and the Attorney General, not for the act of banning the book but for prohibiting its sale and distribution without giving interested parties a chance to defend its publication. The Censorship Board hadn't even notified the IFPA of its decision. I was convinced that the action could be proven unconstitutional.

Mr Justice Hamilton, the judge in the case, referred to the ruling of a Supreme Court case from 1967 related, curiously, to livestock licensing. The principles the Supreme Court had articulated in that case, Justice Hamilton said, made it clear that the Censorship Board had a duty to communicate with authors, editors, or publishers of books and to take into account any defences they might make in favour of the publications.

We won the case and were granted our costs but my family planning colleagues and I weren't the only ones who were pleased at the ruling. 'In one sense, this decision has nothing to do with family planning,' Robin Cochran, the secretary of Family Planning Services, said at a press conference following the ruling. 'It means that the authors of booklets such as this one would have a chance to defend themselves if they came before the Board and hopefully influence a decision.

Other authors whose books had been banned were also happy. The decision meant that they or their publishers and editors could argue that they'd never had the chance to defend their own works in front of the Censorship Board before they'd been banned. The *Irish Press* interviewed a few well-known authors to get their reactions to the ruling, including J.P. Donleavy, whose book, *The Ginger Man*, was banned and Lee Dunne, who had at least five of his works banned, including *Paddy Maguire Is Dead*. Both men were pleased but only Dunne told the *Press* that he actually planned to use the ruling as a basis for a legal action to try to get the ban lifted on his books. Donleavy told the *Press* that the decision was a 'tremendously encouraging development,' and that authors now had a means of defence against the 'arbitrary kind of censorship' the board had imposed. Maybe he thought the legal battle and costs just weren't worth it – but it's also possible that, like me, he knew that having a banned book usually made people want to read it even more and could be more of an asset than a liability in terms of public interest.

About a year after Justice Hamilton's decision, the inevitable appeal of the Attorney General and the Censorship Board reached the Supreme Court, which unanimously upheld the initial decision. The headline in the *Evening Herald* screamed: 'Sex Book Firm's Court Victory', with subheadings reading 'No Porn Flood' and '5000 free copies to be given away'. 'Following today's decision,' the article read, 'all works of literary merit are likely to appear on Irish bookstalls.' I remember being instructed by Mr Rory O'Hanlon (1923-2002), who went on to be one of Ireland's most conservative judges, to look through Trinity College's collection of pornography (needless to say, a restricted section) so I'd be able to compare truly indecent and obscene material with the family planning booklet. Mr O'Hanlon got me a research ticket and off I went. The book I chose to compare our family planning publication to was entitled *Slave to the Whip*. I can't remember if it was ever entered into evidence but no one could have denied that it made our *Family Planning* look like a child's bedtime story.

Pornography was on a lot of conservative minds when the Supreme Court's decision was handed down, as they were worried that the market would now be wide open for the unchecked publication of filth. Mr Justice O'Higgins was quick to point out that wouldn't be the case, stating that in the case of a 'plainly pornographic production,' the censorship board would still be justified in banning the work without notifying publishers, editors or authors. The IFPA's decision to print and distribute 5000 free copies of the booklet all over the country was our way of popping champagne corks in celebration of our victory but we knew there would be other potential court battles. One of the doctors on the IFPA's Executive Committee told the *Herald* that the voluntary fund that had been set aside to pay the costs if we had lost the case would probably be put into cold storage 'for use at a future date on some other issue'.

In 1972, when I was about thirty-six years old, the journalist June Levine (1931-2008) wrote a profile of me in the *Sunday Independent*. Levine was herself a founder member of the Irish Women's Liberation Movement (IWLM), the first and short-lived radical women's rights group in the country. The IWLM staged the famous Contraceptive Train to Belfast in May 1971 in which dozens of women challenged customs officers and the law, by bringing contraceptives from Belfast into Dublin in a public protest. Levine had been on the train and was a passionate and outspoken supporter of legalised contraception for Irish women. She and I were on the same page politically and she painted a flattering picture of me, despite the fact that one of her sub-headings read, 'Rebel or Crank?' It was just the last paragraph that caused uproar in the Crummey house: 'When you ask him how many children he'd have had if he'd been able to plan it, he replies: 'Well, I think I'd have to be honest and say I have two on purpose, three by mistake and I've had a lot of frights.' I had been having coffee with Levine post-interview when she'd casually asked me the question about my kids. I had assumed two things when I'd answered her: first, that she would realise I was joking and second, that it was off the record. When I read the article that Sunday in 1972, I realised I'd been wrong on both counts. We always wanted five children and that's how many we had. Evelyn was always extremely calm about giving birth, so much so that she'd once brought some knitting along to the hospital so she'd have something to do while she was in labour. The nurses were incredulous. 'I don't think we're going to have time for that,' one of them told her.

In the profile, Levine included a mention of the then-new Family Planning Services, Ltd. (FPS), which I had started along with Robin Cochran, Pat O'Donovan, Professor David McConnell, Doctor Derek Freedman, Alan McConnell and a few others from the original IFPA group. It was with this group that we set up a shop called Contraceptives Unlimited in a small property in Harcourt Road. Far from its being a business venture to make money, we opened the shop just to irritate the ministers at the time (the Minister for Health was Charlie Haughey). The thing that kept amazing us was the number of people who came out of the woodwork whenever we provided a new service. Contraceptives Unlimited was supposed to be a symbolic gesture but from the day it opened there were queues of people waiting to get in. We could have made a fortune had we been in it for the money. The distinction was that up until then, we had been distributing contraceptives but now we were deliberately selling them. There was no question but that we were breaking the law; that was, in fact, the point.

Contraceptives Unlimited had been opened for a few weeks when I was at a meeting one night. A journalist I knew well, a medical correspondent, told me he had heard the Gardaí were planning to come in and making arrests in the shop that Tuesday.

'Great!' I said.

As usual when I thought there would be some action with the Gardaí, I rang RTÉ and arranged for cameras to wait in a stake-out in the pub across the street. The woman who was working in the shop that day, Tara O'Kelly, had been instructed that if anyone came in who even remotely resembled a Garda, she was to make it abundantly clear that the shop was breaking the law and give him enough evidence for a conviction.

About half-past three in comes a Garda in uniform. 'Can I have a dozen of those, please?' he asked, pointing at some condoms.

Tara thought, 'This is it, this is the nick!'

'These are a dozen gossamers,' she said, handing them to the Garda. 'They will cost you one pound. I am not distributing them to you. I am selling them to you.' She put them in a bag and took the money and as she took it she repeated, 'I am selling them to you.'

'Shut up, they're for the wife,' the Garda said in irritation.

Eventually, we got annoyed because we had expected the Gardaí or the politicians, to come after us and challenge us but no one did – until a private citizen accused FPS of distributing contraceptives to his daughter, who was of primary school age. He claimed that his young daughter had written me a letter in response to my advertisement in *Woman's Way* and that I had sent her condoms. What he failed to mention was that his 'daughter' had said that she was a married woman with a drunken husband.

Along with other FPS and IFPA directors, I was charged in the District Court with breaching the law by selling and distributing contraceptives. It is rare to see a senior counsel taking a case in the District Court but the FPS got Colm Condon, SC, Donal Barrington SC and Ercus Stewart BL and an additional junior counsel, which in itself was a spectacle. The poor judge on the bench had never in his life seen such an array of legal bodies in front of him. I made an eight-millimetre video of the spectacle outside the court on the day of the case, which included television cameras and protesters on both sides of the contraception issue.

From the opening of the case, it was apparent that the other side was going to have trouble proving that anyone from FPS had broken the law. When the prosecutor called their medical witness and asked him what an IUD was (this was one of the items in question), he said it was either an abortifacient or a contraceptive but when he was asked which, he replied that he didn't know exactly how to classify it.

If the prosecution couldn't define what it was we were charged with distributing, we couldn't be convicted of anything. All eight of us who were charged had instructed our counsel that we would go to prison if convicted rather than simply pay fines. But it didn't arise. I guess a lot of people were disappointed that I didn't land in jail…they could have got rid of me for a day or two!

7

The Social Worker

A crinkled, yellowed photograph of my father shows him resting on the side of Croagh Patrick after burying his first son, also named Frank, who had died shortly after birth. His expression is unreadable. Back then, practicality seemed to trump superstition, especially in the case of a popular and significant family name. It wasn't unusual for names to be recycled for younger children if their older brothers and sisters had died in infancy. My own fifth and last child was a son and there was never any doubt that his name was going to be Frank. My mother was overjoyed by the news that her newest little Crummey grandchild was a male. 'You have a son, you have a son, you have a son,' came the excited announcement after my mother had received the news via telephone that Evelyn had given birth. She ran outside to catch me as I was loading the other children into the car to take them to school.

Young Frank's birth coincided with yet another job change for me. I got more enjoyment and fulfilment out of my voluntary family planning work than from anything having to do with my day job at the post office. The speeches, pickets and media appearances took up so much of my spare time and energy that more than one acquaintance has observed over the years that I could have been a millionaire several times over if I had only focused as much on making money as I had on bringing contraceptives to Ireland or having corporal punishment abolished in schools.

But the one person who never voiced this opinion was the one whose opinion mattered the most. If I handed Evelyn five pounds at the end of the week, she'd say, 'Thanks very much.' If I handed her one hundred and fifty pounds at the end of the next week, she'd say, 'Thanks very much.' She never praised or criticised the amount of money I handed her, because she knew that what I was giving her was all I had. Evelyn was unbelievably laid-back, a quality that I know has more than a little to do with the success of our married life. She knew I wasn't lazy and she was no stranger to hard times herself. Although her father had been a tailor and was never short of work, no one had much money in Kimmage when we were growing up. One day when Evelyn was a baby, her brother pushed her in the pram to the shop and left her outside while he went in for the few items. When he came out, minutes later, she was lying there barefoot. Someone had come along and stolen the shoes right off her tiny feet.

One night, I gave yet another family planning talk in familiar territory, Buswell's Hotel, shocking and, I hope, educating the audience. After I had finished, a woman from the audience approached me but not with the usual tentative, embarrassed manner of someone with a question to ask. Her name was Anne Keogh and she was a case consultant with the Irish Society for the Prevention of Cruelty to Children, (ISPCC). Anne had a career proposition for me: she wondered if I would like to become a social worker with the ISPCC. The organisation would provide the necessary training.

My commitment to Reform and family planning was deepening, as was my opposition to the Catholic Church. The post office wasn't the worst job I'd ever had but the hostility of some of my more devout supervisors was becoming more apparent. I was delighted to get the opportunity to change careers, especially to a job that was so completely people-centred. I did a few interviews with the ISPCC and was very quickly installed in its two-year internal training programme. The fact that I had never had any kind of academic training for such a career didn't worry me at all. I was confident that my education on Kilfenora and as a father of five young children would be more than enough to draw on when I was sent out to give help and advice to other families. On Kilfenora, as a youngster, I had been called on to do basic electrical repairs. Some neighbours asked me to ring from my mother's phone to make funeral arrangements. I had left street football matches to offer to mind Kilfenora babies, at the risk of inviting physical harm from other boys, and as a young adult I had driven a Kilfenora woman in labour to the hospital in the back of my milk lorry. In a way, I think I felt I had always been a social worker; it was just that the ISPCC was the first place ever to offer to pay me for it.

I was paired with the social worker for Ballyfermot, Olive White. I was supposed to do a placement with her first and then other placements with different social workers over the two-year training period but Olive died very suddenly, leaving the ISPCC short a social worker for the area. I would have to learn on the job and take over her caseload much earlier than had been expected.

I worked with two men in Ballyfermot, of whom I formed completely opposite opinions. One was Michael Cleary, the priest who had married Evelyn and me and who was the curate in Ballyfermot. The other was Doctor Paddy Leahy, the local GP, who became a lifelong friend. Doctor Leahy was never off-duty for his patients and, like me, was especially empathetic towards women who were struggling with all sorts of obstacles to try to hold their families and their marriages together. Doctor Leahy was known among the local women as 'the man for the men', meaning that he was willing to step into some ugly situations within marriages if he thought he could help. One woman came to see him one day who was from farther afield than Ballyfermot – his reputation had spread into the surrounding areas. Her husband was in a very bad way, a severe alcoholic, and she had got everyone in to try to set him straight. She was hoping that Doctor Leahy could come to her house to sort him out.

Doctor Leahy arrived at the woman's house to find her husband outrageously drunk in bed. The doctor took the man by the shoulders and shook him roughly, telling him to pull himself together and that he needed to talk to him. He could see the man's bleary eyes, like sluggish marbles, coming into focus.

'You've had everyone to see me,' the man mumbled in the general direction of his wife. 'And now, Picasso.' Which would have been a completely bizarre thing to say if it hadn't often been noted that Paddy Leahy bore a striking resemblance to Pablo Picasso. The doctor fell around the room with laughter. You'd wonder how a man like that would even have known about Picasso. That such wit shone through in such dim and unlikely places as the corporation houses in Ballyfermot in the 1970s is amazing to me but it's quite a Dublin thing.

My experiences with Michael Cleary were much less pleasant and infinitely frustrating. The priest would give me an address, tell me to visit the woman there who might have already had half a dozen children and who had no money and ask me to 'sort her out' with a talk on contraception. Days later, Cleary could be heard on a radio programme toeing the Church's line about the sinfulness of using contraceptives. To me, Cleary's hypocrisy was much worse than if he had disagreed with me outright. At least then I would have known I was dealing with an honest man. The extent of this hypocrisy was revealed to the country long after I worked with Father Cleary when it emerged that he had fathered two children with his unmarried housekeeper.

I had joined the ISPCC at a time when the organisation was still finding its feet. Anne Keogh, who had personally recruited me, left to join the staff of Trinity College and a new case consultant took her place. In the meantime, I was transferred from Ballyfermot into the inner city.

I was beginning to realise that although I loved the work, I had some major differences of opinion with some of the ISPCC management. My first big problem with the agency stemmed from my frequent appearances on radio and television programmes to talk about my work with Reform and family planning. I was on a popular RTÉ programme, *Seven Days*, one night when the topic was annulment. I had told the show's producers beforehand that I wasn't appearing as a spokesperson for the ISPCC, just as a citizen with my own views. But a subtitle appeared every time the camera panned to me – 'Frank Crummey, Social Worker, ISPCC' – that I was unaware of until the next day at work, when I was called in and hauled over the coals by my superiors. They had been particularly upset by my comment that civil divorce should be allowed by Irish law.

Some of my other activities outside work caused further conflict with some of my ISPCC superiors. As a Reform member, I still went to individual schools where parents had reported cases of child abuse and had words with principals and teachers. There were still no laws to protect children against corporal punishment, which made Reform's work at the time all the more important. It wasn't until 1982 that the then Minister for Education, John Boland, formally banned corporal punishment in schools. At a time when parents were so powerless in such situations and the Church had so much influence, Reform's members had to try to protect children by directly confronting the schools. It was a bit of a David-and-Goliath situation. There didn't seem to be any other way to stop the abuse, because we were working way in advance of subsequent changes in the law.

The ISPCC was not happy to hear about my work with Reform. My case consultant told me not to get involved in anything that went on in schools, because the remit of the ISPCC did not extend to schools. I told her that I was against abuse wherever it occurred and to get off my back. I resented the ISPCC's policy because I believed the organisation was ignoring abuse in schools. Maybe it was just too daunting for the organisation to challenge the Christian Brothers and, by association, the Church but I thought that was no excuse. To me, the ISPCC's silence was just another reason why so many children had suffered for so long in schools.

I wasn't exactly hitting it off with my superior but other people in the ISPCC recognised my strengths and started to use them to the organisation's advantage. I had a lot of public speaking experience and I think they appreciated that I could address serious topics and still, at times and where appropriate, be funny. The ISPCC employees in charge of organising the ISPCC AGM in Waterford invited me down to speak on 'battered babies' syndrome, on which I had done a lot of research. It ended up being the most successful AGM in the history of the organisation, which took in more money than ever before in donations on the night I spoke.

This didn't endear me to some of the management. It was becoming increasingly obvious that there was no small amount of resentment, probably born of jealousy, brewing against me. I also realised that I was the exception among my colleagues in ways that extended beyond political ideology. Many of them, no matter how well-intentioned, were extremely young and green, just out of college. Young men and women in their early twenties, they had little real-world experience, yet they were working in a profession in which it was their daily job to visit and advise married couples and parents in crisis. A lot of them were bewildered by what they saw and heard but were too proud to come back to the office and ask their case consultants or their older colleagues for advice. I was nothing if not streetwise, a trait that had first surfaced in my instinct for knowing which Brothers to keep away from in school.

One young social worker stood out because she had such a

different attitude. Eavanne O'Donoghue was just as young and just as green as her colleagues but she was never afraid to ask for assistance, a quality I found fabulous and extremely endearing. She was assigned to the Ballymun area when she started out with the ISPCC, so I helped her. She was a fast learner and we were fast friends: we'd go out on home visits together. One day we stopped into a beautiful luxury sweet shop called Conway's in my old neighbourhood. The Conways were friendly with Evelyn and her family and I could see Mrs Conway looking at me and thinking, 'Does she know he's married?' Eventually she couldn't hold back and said, 'Frank, how's Evelyn and the children?' I found it comforting that the people we knew always watched out for one another and made sure there was no funny business going on.

Before long, I would ring Eavanne if I felt I needed back-up for something and she would do the same, an arrangement that was rare in the ISPCC at the time. The main reason Eavanne learned so quickly was her willingness to ask questions and her acceptance that she would be making mistakes and probably lots of them at first.

Some of Eavanne's questions were serious and I answered them seriously. But some of them were hilarious and I answered these with the enjoyment and irreverence they deserved. One of her million-pound questions was about the 'penis in a thousand'.

Eavanne had a crisis case one Friday – crises always seemed to happen on a Friday afternoon, never on a Monday – when she was called out to a house in Ballymun by a abused wife. Her husband had beaten her earlier that day and left the house but she was afraid he'd be ready for another round when he returned. She told Eavanne that her sister, her sister's partner and their two children lived in the house with them and Eavanne was satisfied that they would be able to keep her from being seriously hurt. She told the abused woman to bring her husband to the ISPCC office the following Monday morning for counselling, doubting that they'd ever show up. Miraculously, Monday morning dawned to find the couple waiting in the office. Eavanne and I split them up – the wife with Eavanne, the husband with me.

'You really ruined my Friday afternoon,' I said to the husband. When I questioned him about his home life and his wife's sister and the sister's partner, I realised that the partner's name was familiar to me. Then it dawned on me why it was familiar and I told Eavanne that if she accomplished nothing else in that house, she should convince the wife's sister to use some form of contraception.

It turned out I had encountered the sister's partner on a case I had worked on in Dún Laoghaire, in a house he shared with his wife and four children. They were now separated and I was working on a maintenance order for the wife, who was seeking financial support from him. If the same man was now living with another woman with additional children in another troubled household, the best thing we could do for everyone involved was to make sure we slowed his rate of reproduction.

Eavanne soon found that it wasn't going to be that easy. When she spoke to his new partner about contraception, the woman told Eavanne that she had already discovered the pill wouldn't work for her because she had a heart murmur that the pill would aggravate. When Eavanne started explaining other contraceptive options to her, she baulked as well. Apparently she had discussed using an IUD with her partner and he had informed her nonchalantly that it wouldn't work because he had 'a penis in a thousand', that was so big it would knock the coil out of place.

Eavanne wasn't really sure how to respond to this information. She was fairly sure there was some cause for scepticism but she knew she was only learning about most sexual matters. For all she knew, it was possible that this man really did have some kind of freaky anatomy and was legitimately restricted in his contraceptive options. She didn't know for sure but she knew the first person to ask.

I nearly choked with laughter when Eavanne found me in Buswell's Hotel with some of our other colleagues and asked me if there was any possibility the man's story could be true. 'Eavanne, love,' I said, 'It's all right. He's only boasting. I hope she doesn't have any false teeth in danger of being knocked out, too.'

Shortly afterwards, several other social workers and I were in court when the proud owner of the penis in a thousand showed up for the hearing on his maintenance order for his wife and four children in Dún Laoghaire. By now word had got around and the story had attained legendary status. We whispered to one another that this was the man himself. Giggling reverberated around the chamber and the judge silenced us by looking up sharply and asking, irritated, what was so funny. He was genuinely curious and didn't like being left out of a joke in his own courtroom, so after the proceedings had finished he strode from the bench over to us and demanded to know what we'd been laughing at. He couldn't help cracking a smile himself when he heard.

Time and again, I saw people, mostly women, torturing themselves over the contradictions between the Church's rules about sex and marriage and what they felt they needed to do for themselves in order to have more enjoyable and fulfilling lives. In the Church's eyes, it was wrong for married women who already had families that were too large for them to manage to use contraception. But continuing to have children would cripple some of them financially or physically. If they decided knowingly to go against the Church's teachings, the way they had lived their lives for so long lost much of its meaning but if they kept following the Church, they were condemning themselves to lives of continuing hardship and sacrifice that would only become harder to bear.

One such woman whose case was referred to me by a colleague had got married later in life and had a child with her husband. When I first met her, her husband was staying out late at night, drinking, coming home and occasionally striking her. I had learned over the years not to trivialise any domestic violence but this woman's injuries weren't serious. After I had seen her several times, she confessed to me that she was distraught because she was sure she was 'living in sin'.

'Does it have to do with your marriage?' I asked.

'Yes,' she said. She explained that although she had been in her early forties when she married her husband, she was, of course, a virgin. It had taken her a while to get used to things but she enjoyed the intimacy of sex with him. The trouble had started when he asked her to change positions, with her on top instead. They were both convinced that it was a 'sinful' position but he kept asking her to do it anyway. She had conceived her child that way and was convinced that she had conceived in a sinful position. She felt so guilty that she had stopped going to Confession and although she still went to Mass, she had stopped receiving Communion because she had stopped going to Confession. Now her child was getting to the age that she was worried he would notice that everyone else was receiving Communion except her and this caused her great embarrassment and anxiety.

I tried to explain to her that the object of being a loving partner in a marriage was to give your spouse pleasure and as long as no one was being forced to do anything they weren't comfortable with, there was nothing sinful about it. But I could tell my reassurances weren't going to mean much when she asked, 'Mr Crummey, are you a Catholic?' If I said no, I knew she wouldn't take anything I'd said seriously. But if I said yes, I'd be lying and I didn't want to do that, either. So I thought of a compromise that might work. 'Hold on, love,' I said. 'I know a lovely priest who will hear your Confession and everything will be fine.' The priest I had in mind was Brian D'Arcy, a Passionist who had been through Mount Argus and who I knew to be a compassionate, tolerant and, perhaps most importantly, quite liberal man.

I arranged for the woman to meet Father D'Arcy and things went according to my plan. The priest backed me up and the woman's life changed dramatically for the better. Her husband stopped staying out late at night. He stopped his heavy drinking and stopped hitting her. She sent me a beautiful box of chocolates for my help and found the courage to say to me the next time we met that she was now oversexed. I was thrilled things had worked out for her but couldn't help thinking about the thousands of other women like her who didn't have someone to help them free themselves from their guilt and self-torment. Their suffering radiated from the Church's teachings like ripples around a stone thrown into a lake.

During the three years I was a social worker, I gained a reputation as a man to call who would sort things out, even if a problem arose after hours. Although I had a tendency to confront men who were much bigger than me, I had learned that it was nearly always a good idea to have someone bigger on my side as backup. Many nights, Syl Collins found himself drafted into voluntary service as my unofficial bodyguard without really remembering exactly when he had agreed to it.

One night Syl and I were leaving my house to play snooker when the phone rang. It was the editor of a women's magazine to say that a woman from the north side of Dublin had called her, desperate for help. Her husband was beating her very badly. The editor had rung around making enquiries as to who would be willing to go out to the house and she had come up with my name and number.

'Sorry, we're not playing snooker,' I said to Syl.

We headed out to a nice housing estate in north County Dublin and found the address. It was obvious that the man who opened the door was a Garda. 'I'd like to talk to your wife,' I said to him. I knew it was essential that I get the woman to a neighbour's house where we could talk and the sooner the better.

When Syl, the woman and I got to the neighbours' house, she showed me her injuries. There wasn't a part of her body from her neck to the back of her knees that wasn't covered in bruises. I told her I would take her to the hospital for a check-up and then to the women's refuge if that was what she wanted. She launched into an almost apologetic explanation about her husband's treatment of her. 'He doesn't drink or smoke,' she said. But if he came home in the mid-afternoon from his 6am shift at work and went straight to the phone to disconnect it, shut the windows and turned up the radio, she knew she was in trouble. He would beat her with anything from his baton to a hurley or a belt, for absolutely no reason.

I was driving a two-door Ford Escort and the woman came outside with me and got into my car. Just as I closed the passenger door, I saw the woman's husband, in full uniform, coming down the street on his motorbike: a big man, much bigger than me and obviously violent. He jumped off the bike and threatened me, telling me to get his wife out of the car. I said he'd have to smash the window to get her out and if he did that, he'd lose his job. Syl was close by, keeping a watchful eye over everything. The neighbour wisely stepped in and asked the Garda to come into the house to talk while his wife sat in my car.

Once inside the house, the Garda sat down across from me and glared. I could tell he was barely able to restrain himself from attacking me. Syl stood in the background by the fire, stuffing a poker in and out of it in silent rhythm. Finally, in annoyance, the man asked him what he was doing. 'It's like this,' Syl said in his usual bright, brassy voice. 'If you get up off that chair and go near my mate, I'll shove this up your arse.'

I knew I had a good wing man and I couldn't help but notice that some daring part of Syl secretly enjoyed himself on these crusades. Our very first exchange when we met as boys in Bolton Street Tech began with my threatening him and his twin brother but ever since then we had been on the same side. We got the woman safely to the women's refuge that night but on the morning her case was to be heard in the High Court she told me she loved her husband and she wanted to go back to him, which she did. I knew by then that I could only help people as much as they wanted to be helped.

Soon afterwards, I began receiving anonymous, mildly annoying letters, that always started off with the greeting 'Dear Fruit and Nutcase'. I wouldn't have had much difficulty figuring out who sent them even if the sender hadn't used a specific Garda term, referring to me as a little 'latchiko'. I can't remember the exact meaning of the insult but 'bollocks' is close enough. I took them to my local Garda station where the sergeant told me those types of letters were usually very hard to trace. I said there wouldn't be any need for a trace because I knew who was sending them.

'You won't get another one,' the sergeant told me and I didn't.

I was still working in the inner-city area when I was called in one day to ask for my advice on a difficult case that one of the other social workers was in charge of in a wealthy part of south Dublin. It made sense that individual social workers were assigned to certain areas of the city depending on how well the ISPCC thought they would fit in with their own backgrounds. I had no problem with that arrangement but I knew they would never have assigned me to this particular area. It was one of the wealthiest areas of Dublin and the social worker there was a graduate with a posh accent. The problem was that the children in the house hadn't been seen by the social worker assigned to the case. The ISPCC's policy was that children had to be seen within twenty-four hours of a complaint and the neighbours had been reporting that they suspected the children were being very badly beaten.

I said I'd go out and talk to the next-door neighbours who had made the reports. When I did, alarm bells started going off everywhere. The neighbours told me the children could be heard 'screaming reluctantly'. I left the neighbours, went right over to the house and banged on the door. I got no response at all from inside the house.

I went to court and made an application for a search warrant for the house. The judge was just about to sign when he realised it was a posh address and he told me to go and have another try. It was sort of a reverse discrimination that I had encountered before in the courts, whereby judges were hesitant to let social workers interfere in the affairs of the wealthy. I knew there was no time to waste, so I went into another court with a different judge and got my warrant.

About a week went by and I became aware that nothing had happened when, on a Sunday afternoon, I got a phone call at home from the next-door neighbour of the family, whom I had interviewed before I got the search warrant. She had somehow managed to track my number down.

'My husband and I have agreed that I'll make one more attempt to save the lives of the children,' she said, telling me that screams could still be heard from the house. I told her I was very sorry that nothing had yet been done and that I'd try to put things right immediately.

I knew the children in that house were in serious danger and when I said this to my superiors, they asked me to deal with the case. The next morning, I started working early, because I expected that it would take me the better part of the day to arrange everything to adhere to the terms of the search warrant before I could actually enter the house. I was required to have a doctor and a Garda of the rank of sergeant with me when I went to the house. I contacted the local Gardai and informed them that I'd be needing someone later that day. They were reluctant to help until I made it clear that I wasn't just asking for someone, I was telling them I needed them. I left them with the address and the time to meet me there. I then went around from doctor to doctor, looking for someone who was willing to come out to the house that night. No one would agree to come with me. Finally, I met a lovely Doctor McKenna who I offered to pay in advance out of my own pocket if he was willing to come that night. 'Not at all, I'm a family man,' he said. 'What time do you want me there?' In between finding a Garda and a doctor, I also rang a friend and fellow-social worker, Brigid Barry. She offered to come along with me for support and I didn't turn her down.

I knew if I made a mistake with this case, the ISPCC would have my guts for garters. So I thought it best to arrive early on my own and go to the next-door neighbours' house to get my bearings. I sat on their stairs with my dictaphone and recorded what I expected to find. I knew the children would be injured, probably with blunt instruments. I also expected to see a case of communicated insanity between the parents and I had come ready with the pink forms that were necessary for committing people for psychiatric treatment. All the others – the sergeant, the doctor and Brigid – began to arrive, and it was time to approach the house. If it had been Ballyfermot or Crumlin and Garda vehicles appeared, there would have been a mill of children and neighbours around the house. In this wealthy part of south Dublin, gates were closing discreetly but faces were appearing in windows all around. If something unpleasant was about to happen, the neighbours wanted to see it – but only from a distance.

When we first knocked and told the man we had a warrant to enter, he replied through the door that he was the king of his castle. We tried talking to him through the sitting-room window, where we could at least get a better look at him. He wanted me to pass the warrant through the letterbox to him but I refused and instead held it up to the window for him to read. I told him that if he didn't let us in, I'd have no choice but to break the sitting room window and climb in, which is what I ended up doing. The Garda and I climbed in through the window but we found ourselves quite alone in the sitting room and discovered that the man had locked us in.

We didn't want to do any more damage to the house than was absolutely necessary but we had to get to the children somehow. I remembered the wheel brace in the boot of my car. The Garda and I climbed back out the broken window and I got the brace, went back to the front door and forced it open.

In the front hall was this huge man with a schizo tremor to beat the band. You'd have certified him going past you on a bicycle. The man's size and obvious state of mental deterioration were a sight and everyone was worried about his reaction turning violent. Surprisingly, he was polite enough and he invited all four of us – me, the Garda, the doctor and Brigid – into the sitting room he had locked us into only moments earlier, after the Garda and I had smashed his front window.

I said I wanted to see his children.

'You cannot see them,' he replied. 'They're abusing themselves in the spirit and will have to be slain.' He then turned to Brigid, the doctor and the Garda in turn and said to each of them, 'You're lustful and an evil spirit.' He repeated the phrase until he got to me and to me he said, 'You're not lustful, you're just violent.'

'Look, it's very simple,' I said. 'Either you introduce me to your children or I'll break down every bedroom door until I find them.' With that, the man's wife came down the stairs, wearing a maxi dress and quoting St Paul to the Corinthians. My heart sank: she was obviously in as bad a state as her husband. But the man did bring me up the stairs and opened one of the bedroom doors to reveal the children. They looked like they ranged in age from fifteen down to about six. He directed his children to say hello.

'Hello,' they all said, in robotic unison.

The doctor had to examine the children and he took one of the boys out of the room. His backside was a mass of congealed blood, as hard as marble.

At that, Brigid was very upset. The young sergeant was nearly crying. He wanted to go for the guy himself and it was bedlam. I had brought the pink forms the psychiatric hospital needed to commit someone and I had the man's form already signed by the necessary people – a close relative and a GP. I had been to see the man's sister earlier that day and she had signed. But now I realised I needed one for the woman, too. I signed Frank Crummey, next of kin, and I told the doctor to put his name on it and off they went. As she was getting into the ambulance, the woman turned and gave a brief diatribe on pornography before turning to me and saying, 'Won't you feed the dog?' The couple was taken to the hospital under Garda escort and I went back upstairs to the children. I told them gently that their parents were going away for a rest because they were very tired and that they were at the hospital. I said I would have to bring them all to the hospital too for a check-up.

'We cannot leave until we hear our father's voice,' one of the eldest boys told me in the same mechanical voice. 'He knows all, he sees all, he sees us in the spirit.' The rest of them just sat there, motionless. But I noticed one of the older children was looking at me.

'Look, love, you can't stay here like this,' I said.

'Are they gone?' she asked.

'Yes,' I said.

'I'm getting a case. We're going and you're coming with us,' she said to her brother. I could tell that she was the only one who hadn't been utterly trapped by the terrible physical and emotional abuse of her parents.

I regularly picked up night-shift work, from eight to midnight, as a switchboard operator at a Dublin hospital while I was a social worker and Eavanne O'Donoghue did the same. She was covering my shift that night and had known about the difficulties of the case. I rang her and told her what was going on and she offered to send an ambulance for the children. But then I thought it would be less traumatic for the children, whose parents had just been taken away in ambulances, to go in private cars. Getting the children into the cars was easy enough but once they arrived at the hospital, some of them wouldn't get out. 'We cannot move until we hear our father's voice,' they repeated mechanically. The Gardaí had to take them out by force.

The hospital staff was extremely gentle and understanding and a ward was sectioned off for the six children. When a doctor took me to look in on them as they slept at around one o'clock that morning, I noticed that they all slept with their hands outside the bed covers. It turned out that their father did a nightly inspection of their hands and if their hands were under the covers it was assumed they were masturbating. That guaranteed a beating. They were also expected to assist with their own beatings in some way, which all of them except the girl did – that system explained the 'reluctant' screams the neighbours had heard. The beatings the children had received had been extremely severe.

After this case, things changed for me at work. Once I had forced my way into the house and the children's horrific injuries had been revealed, everyone at the ISPCC realised that I had rightly predicted the seriousness – and urgency – of the case. I have no doubt that if the family had been left alone, some or all of the six children wouldn't have survived. We had gone into the house in early August. A psychiatrist at the ISPCC case conference afterwards said that he thought the chances were very high that a homicide would have occurred in the house by 15 August, because it was the feast of the Assumption.

The case of those children was one of my most difficult and emotionally exhausting cases but even though my colleagues had a new respect for me, my career in social work still had its difficulties. Like all the other social workers, I had to complete placements in different areas of the city as part of my training. But my superiors had found that I was exceptionally hard to place. They'd put my name forward and suddenly available places would have been filled. Eventually I told them not to worry – I could find my placements myself.

I was working out in Ballymun on a placement in a psychiatric clinic with an excellent psychiatrist, Brian McCaffrey, when I learned about the importance of choosing my words extremely carefully when talking to vulnerable people. Usually I was expected to sit in with Doctor McCaffrey and a patient, say nothing and then talk to the doctor about what I had observed after the patient left. One day, a woman came in and I realised I knew her. To signal to the doctor that I knew her, I said to the woman, 'Good morning, Joan,' as she sat down.

She began telling the doctor about her problems. Occasionally, her husband would come home at night, beat her very badly and then immediately go to bed after taking an overdose of pills. She would ring for the ambulance and they'd take him away to have his stomach pumped. Her split lips, black eyes and other injuries were usually ignored because her husband had just overdosed. The doctor told her that if her husband was still very bad within the next few days, he'd send a psychiatric nurse from St Brendan's to her house to do what she could. He turned to me and asked if I had anything I'd like to say to Joan.

'Joan, why do you ring for the ambulance?' I asked.

Several nights later, Joan's husband came home, beat her, left her in bits, then took his usual overdose and went to bed. So did Joan. She had a good night's sleep and her husband was dead in the morning. The Gardaí came to her house with the ambulance, this time to take her husband's body away. When the Gardaí questioned her about why she hadn't rung for the ambulance this time, she told them that the social worker she had talked to that week had told her not to.

Doctor McCaffrey stood firm, something I've never forgotten. He told the Gardaí that he had been in the room at the time and that Joan had been mistaken. I had indeed asked her why she rang for the ambulance but I had never said not to do it.

The most disturbing cases that I ever came across were those involving sexual abuse of children within families. But in some ways it's difficult to identify any one case as being more horrible than the last or the next. There were so many more people suffering, most of them women and children, than the general population could ever fathom. Abuse took place behind closed doors, like a subculture of its own, rarely spilling into the streets or anywhere other people could see it, so most people were completely ignorant of its existence. I saw a house with twenty children, most of them the mother's and a few who belonged to the elder daughters. They were all the father's, who was in prison. There was so much dirt that when I knocked on the windowpane, my finger stuck to the glass and the mother had a dirty bucket on the table out of which she was scooping cups of tea. There were many more cases of abused wives who had no chance of ever being able to look after their children properly because of their own injuries, fear and depression. I saw Eavanne held at knife-point by someone she was trying to help. There seemed to be no limit to people's potential for cruelty, especially towards their own family and children.

As much as possible, though, amidst all the angst and desperation I saw on a daily basis, I kept my senses finely tuned and receptive to kindness and humour. My sensibilities lean towards the darkest kind of gallows humour that can still be considered funny but I think it forms a deep, stabilising undercurrent of my personality. I was aware that I could be repelled by the horrors I encountered at work in the morning and just as easily astounded by someone's capacity for compassion in the afternoon. That was the way the world worked – through a tangle of contradictions. Nowhere were those contradictions more apparent than in social work.

Every month the executive board of the ISPCC met and

a different social worker or case consultant went along to tell them about his or her work. The board was mostly made up of wealthy do-gooders who volunteered to help raise money for the organisation to supplement government funding. Most of the other social workers who had spoken in front of the board had simply reported how many cases they'd opened and closed in the past weeks, leaving out all the unsavoury details. I didn't think that did anyone any good. If these people were spending their time raising funds for the ISPCC, I thought it was fair that they should know exactly how the money they raised was being used. Instead of giving an account of my work by the numbers, I simply told them what I had done and seen, at work during the previous several days. By the time I had finished the short talk, several of the board members were in tears.

Some people find the dark roots of their own sense of humour in fear or tragedy. I think I do too and I had a lot of raw material to work with in my job experiences. But no matter how resilient I thought I was, finding so many broken people at the lowest points in their lives began to affect me. Somewhere inside me a scale of sorts was being tipped toward despair and its weight was increasing fast.

8

THE BREAKDOWN

Five children, my job as a social worker, my second job as a switchboard operator, my family planning and Reform activities at night and occasional weekend trips across the border to collect thousands of condoms kept me occupied in the early 1970s. For the first time since I'd been driving buses in London, I genuinely enjoyed going to work every day. The difference was that with London Bus, I finished my shift for the night, went home, and didn't think any more about work until I climbed back into the bus the next morning. In social work, my clients' stories, faces and circumstances haunted me.

The case I worked on that got the most media attention had the most tragic outcome:: I was responsible for placing a little boy in Madonna House, which was run by the Sisters of Charity. He was between five and six years old when he arrived at Madonna House. He became the responsibility of the sisters of Madonna House and the social worker there, who was an ex-De La Salle brother. As the child's seventh birthday grew near, the social worker kidnapped him. He brought him over to Edinburgh, spent a week with him in a nice hotel, then strangled him. The social worker's logic for the murder was apparently to guarantee the child's eternal redemption. He figured that since the age of seven is commonly accepted as the point at which children reach the ability to use reason, the child would also soon be tempted to commit sin. He would probably end up in prison for the rest of his life and then go to hell. This way, if he strangled the little boy before he became a sinner, he would be guaranteed to get into heaven instead.

Naturally, the nation was shocked. The child's mother was devastated and made statements to the effect that he had been taken away from her in the first place because she was a widow. My solicitors issued a statement saying that I would welcome a public enquiry into the case because I had nothing to hide and nothing to apologise for, other than that the child had ended up in Madonna House and in contact with such a dangerous, deranged man. I knew I wasn't responsible for the boy's death but in the end, I hadn't been able to protect him.

I was working around the clock. The concept of the nine-to-five work day just did not fit with what I felt were the demands of my job. If I wasn't going out to visit clients, giving a talk on family planning or operating the hospital switchboard on the night shift, I was doing extra tasks for the ISPCC, completely immersed emotionally in the work. I heard about the ISPCC's fundraising effort toward the goal of buying a double-decker bus to use as a children's playschool. The fundraiser in charge of the project was planning on selling raffle tickets for small prizes for the price of twopence each. I knew that at that rate it would be years before they raised the money. I was fairly confident I could do it myself in one night and all entirely legally at that. I went to Des Hand, the ISPCC executive director, and asked if he minded if I gave it a try.

I knew it was a matter of asking the right people who were in a position to be able to donate the amount of money we needed. I arranged to get myself invited to speak to the Round Table, a well-known philanthropic group, at the St Lawrence Hotel in Howth. I told them the purpose of the bus and who it was for and they said they'd fund it. The ISPCC was thrilled. It would be one of the last tasks I did as an ISPCC employee. Shortly afterwards,

I checked myself into the Kylemore Nursing Home, suffering from anxiety, at the beginning of a nervous breakdown.

From when I was very young, I loved to run. I ran all over the neighbourhood and when I was old enough I ran in road races. I've run marathons in different cities, including the Boston Marathon. I never had much finesse or style but I made up for that with pure endurance and stamina. I know something about pain and pushing myself to my limits physically. When I applied some of the rules of running to the rest of my life, I found that they didn't make the transition well at all. It may have been natural to burn all my physical energy in a road race to the point of exhaustion but if I did the same at work or as an activist, it was much harder to build it back, emotionally. I was drained and distressed and I needed help.

Doctor Jim Loughran, a good friend of mine by now from the family planning groups, knew the psychiatrist at the Kylemore Clinic, Doctor Tim McCracken, and he was the one who gave me a referral. Evelyn and another friend of mine drove me to the nursing home. The Kylemore, which was run by the Methodist Church, was state-of-the-art and very expensive. Even in the midst of my anxiety, the thought was preying in the back of my mind: how I was going to afford this kind of care, especially as I had no health insurance.

When you have a nervous breakdown, very often it's more stressful on your family than it is on you. And I was crying and the lot. But I thought then: am I going to have more of these nervous breakdowns or am I going to have no more. And if I was going to have no more, I knew I was going to have to adjust my lifestyle.

I was in the Kylemore for three weeks. Shortly after my admission, Doctor McCracken told me they'd had a committee meeting and they'd decided to have me as their guest. They knew I couldn't afford them. That was absolutely fantastic. It wouldn't have happened anywhere else. I liked Doctor McCracken very much but for the most part I made the decision that I could counsel myself after I got myself back together and through the worst of things.

I also decided it was time to identify the things in my life that were causing me the most stress. I was obviously working too much, strictly in terms of hours. But I was also becoming too emotionally involved with my clients and I knew it. I saw desperate people every day but I had to accept that I couldn't fix the problems of every single family. I also had to clarify for myself what my real feelings were about the Catholic Church, whose policies towards sex, women and other cultural issues I had been openly criticising now for years – and also my real feelings about God and religion itself. It was a lot to reflect upon over the course of a few weeks.

While I was in the nursing home, I tried to stay true to my old self and my personality. Even a nervous breakdown couldn't entirely stifle my sense of fun and serendipity. I was sitting with some of the other patients one morning, waiting to see Doctor McCracken. The nurses were making smalltalk with the patients, asking us about our favourite singers and songs. Some of the other patients were naming the popular entertainers of the day but I wasn't really joining in the conversation. They would have heard of my favourite singer, who was very famous, but maybe not of my favourite song. I wasn't that taken with pop culture. When a nurse asked me, I told her as much but she pressed me.

'All right, it's 'The Fairy Tree', sung by John McCormack,' I said. John McCormack (1884-1945) was an Irish tenor with an operatic voice who sang ballads and traditional songs. A very old woman sitting across from me who had been off in her own world, not paying a bit of attention to the conversation, suddenly perked up.

'I wrote that song,' she said.

Heads turned towards her in amazement. I was sceptical. I

was, after all, in a psychiatric home and the chances that this group of people would be having this exact conversation in the presence of the woman who had written my favourite song seemed outlandish, to say the least. But whimsy got the better of me. Anyway, things like this seemed to have a habit of happening to me.

'What's your name?' I asked the woman.

'Miss Leslie,' she replied.

Now I wasn't sure. I knew the woman who wrote 'The Fairy Tree' used the pen name Temple Lane but I had never heard what her real name was. I knew someone who *would* know, though. I asked the nurse for the phone and dialled RTÉ to get Donncha Ó Dúlaing, a radio presenter whose programme I had appeared on many times.

'Donncha, you'll never guess who I think I've got here,' I said excitedly.

'Hello, Frank, how are you? I heard you haven't been well,' Donncha said.

'Never mind that. What was Temple Lane's real name?'

When Donncha confirmed that Temple Lane's real name was indeed Isabel Leslie, I told him he had to come in to the Kylemore and do an interview with her. Donncha was excited too. This was an intriguing story. No one really knew what had happened to Temple Lane and it would be interesting to find out about her life. Donncha came in with his equipment and interviewed Miss Leslie, from whom thirty years and a lifetime of worry seemed to melt away. She was even confident enough to haggle with Donncha over payment for the interview, making him raise her fee from £15 to £25 pounds.

Meeting Miss Leslie was the nicest thing that happened to me at the nursing home. The worst was the visit of one of my ISPCC superiors. Apparently she had stopped in for the friendly, collegial purpose of saying hello and seeing how I was feeling. Unfortunately, the conversation turned to work and my superior told me straight out that I would never work as a social worker again. She then suggested, almost as an afterthought, that I might be able to drive the playschool bus, for which I had recently raised the funds single-handedly.

I left the Kylemore feeling better than when I went in but in fairness, that wasn't saying much. I knew that making the changes in my life that I had decided upon while in the hospital was going to be the hard part. I knew my days at the ISPCC were numbered and although they hadn't yet sacked me they did so shortly afterwards. It wasn't the fact that they sacked me that surprised me so much as their reasoning for it. My mental health wasn't mentioned. It seemed that certain members of the executive board felt that it was 'inconsistent' for a good social worker to be a strong advocate of family planning. I found a searing, knife-twisting sort of hypocrisy in the fact that I was supplying several of the board members themselves with contraceptives at the time.

Although my being sacked was unfair, I wasn't that surprised. Several years earlier, at the end of my first year with the ISPCC, I had been awarded first prize, and a cheque for £100, for receiving the highest marks on the society's in-service training course. There was a dinner and a ceremony where the top three achievers were to be congratulated and presented with their cheques. I was chatting away to my friends and colleagues when one of my superiors pulled me aside.

'Frank,' she said, 'I have to let you know that Mr Whelan is not prepared to shake hands with you today.' Mr Whelan was the Vice-President of the National Executive of the ISPCC.

'Why?' I asked.

'Because he doesn't want to shake hands with someone who has handled condoms,' she said.

I took my cheque and a few friends and went off to the hotel bar, where I had my customary mineral. The photograph that appeared in the paper the next day showed the second and third-place winners smiling and shaking hands with Mr Whelan, with no mention of the first-place winner at all.

Around the same time, I had been called in for a meeting with a member of the ISPCC's executive board. When I sat down, the representative told me the board had agreed that they were unhappy with the fact that I was a director of Family Planning Services. He asked me to swap Evelyn's name for my own on the FPS's list of directors. Naturally, I was offended and said I had no intention of doing this. The thing that had disgusted me most about the meeting was that throughout the discussion, the board member kept reassuring me that he agreed with everything I and FPS stood for and were trying to accomplish. It reminded me of the kind of rank hypocrisy that Father Michael Cleary had displayed in publicly renouncing contraceptives while privately asking me to advocate their use and to educate women about them.

With five children to support and no job, I had to think, and quickly, what my next job was going to be. The blow of being sacked was softened slightly by the visit of the ISPCC's executive director, Des Hand, to my house. Des told me he felt terrible about my being sacked and asked if I would be interested in coming back to work directly for him as an administrative assistant. In that kind of position, I might have had more of a say in how things were run than when I was a social worker out in the field. I would definitely have taken the job if Des Hand hadn't left the job himself shortly afterwards!

We had no money and I needed to do something. When my friend Syl Collins visited our house, he would grab Evelyn dramatically as if to hug and kiss her, something he liked doing anyway, shove twenty pounds into her bra and run out the door. He wanted to be generous but he didn't want to get any thanks for it – just give the money and go home. Syl didn't want to embarrass us by putting us in the position of having to accept anything from him. If he just shoved it into Evelyn's bra, she had to take it. He also brought a big sack overflowing with toys for the kids at Christmas, a gesture that was all the sweeter because he had little idea what kinds of presents to buy for little girls. Other friends and family members also made sure we were looked after. June Levine, who was working on *The Late Late Show*, sent me a bag of lovely new toys after the Christmas *Toy Show*. Nuala O'Faolain was also very kind, giving me building work to do in her home.

I finally decided on a two-fold approach for the following year that included going to college and working nights as a private detective. Since my years at Bolton Street were the last time I had seen the inside of a classroom, I thought it would be good for me to go back to college and work towards a degree. I enrolled in Trinity College's sociology course as a mature student and started my own one-man PI operation, Irish Investigative Consultants, with an office in Kilbarrack. The standard practice of tacking 'Investigative Consultants' on to a surname, wouldn't, for obvious reasons, work for me. 'Crummey Investigative Consultants' wasn't the most confidence-inspiring of company names.

Despite the exciting portrayals of suave, tough private detectives in the films, my new professional life was not glamorous. It mostly involved following husbands (or wives) suspected of cheating but there were a few other cases of some variety, including one that involved an investigation of jewel fraud for an insurance company. In social work, I had been trying to help families to stick together and work through their problems, while with my PI work I was often asked to supply the information that would break the family apart for good. I may only have been the messenger but even so, it was no fun bearing such unpleasant news.

Often, I would need to do night work that involved trailing people to bars and clubs around town, trying to catch them in the act of infidelity. I knew I was far too conspicuous an observer as a man on my own, so I made a practice of bringing along 'molls' with me for cover. This suited me just fine; after all, this kind of work had to be more of a laugh if I could bring along a partner and I always preferred to have someone to chat to. I recruited women who were friends or former colleagues and one of my favourites was Imelda McCarthy, a fellow, like-minded social worker. Imelda and I frequently posed as sweethearts in dark corners of smoky pubs in order to keep an eye on our subjects.

There was another moll I brought along with me who managed to get us both into outrageous situations. One night I was out with her and we were having trouble tracking down the man we were looking for on another standard infidelity case. We went to the first pub we thought he might be in and I had my usual orange mineral, while my moll had a vodka tonic. But there was no sign of the man we were looking for. We went on to another place and had the same round of drinks and this time we did end up finding our man. By the time we got to the third bar and my moll was into her third vodka tonic, our man was hitting on her. I saw her make her way to the loo and the man slipping out of the bar after her. Minutes later I found them outside, rolling around in the flower bed together in the throes of drunken passion, right beside the main Dublin-Belfast road. I grabbed my moll, who by this time was extremely drunk, and placed her in the passenger's seat in the car. She slid off the seat.

'You're not getting paid for tonight,' I said to her as we drove off – although this was one way to prove that the man was really a cheat.

I was surrounded by all these mad people, yet *I* was seen as the outrageous one. Even though my night-time activities were unorthodox and I was one of the most outspoken advocates of contraception and critics of the Catholic Church, I was also a husband and father. In my family life, I was quite conservative, especially compared to many of my friends and acquaintances.

I had a case where a wife would hire me to watch her husband because she knew he had hired someone to watch her, just to be 'even'. There was no other logic to it but it wasn't all that uncommon for both people in the marriage to be having affairs, as in this case. This woman arranged to meet me one afternoon in Jury's Hotel, where I was eating one of my favourites, Chicken Maryland. When she spotted me she sat down across from me and produced a pair of knickers from her handbag. She told me she wanted me to take them back to my laboratory and test them for sperm. I'm thinking, for God's sake, will you just let me eat my Chicken Maryland. It was funny that anyone could have thought I was running a business sophisticated enough to have a laboratory.

One of my other all-time favourite clients was a fabulously wealthy man named Ed. At first, Ed's case sounded just like scores of other cases I had worked on – he wanted someone to follow his wife. But Ed's motivation wasn't suspicion. It was irritation. He hadn't been getting on with his wife and although he had no reason to think she was being unfaithful, he wanted to annoy her by having someone follow her.

I thought Ed was mad. But money was money and Ed had plenty that he seemed not to know what to do with. The day he hired me, he produced a wad of notes from his pocket and began peeling them off. I was so fixated by the huge roll of cash that the numbers on the notes I was being handed didn't really register with me. I do remember telling Ed I'd look after what he needed as I robotically put the pounds in my pocket. In my car, as I regained my senses, I took out the notes and discovered they were all – three of them or so – hundred pound notes. On my way home, I stopped at a shop to buy Evelyn a washing machine. Over the next little while, Ed's eccentricities kept me in the clover, which suited me down to the ground: nobody was getting hurt and I was getting paid – for the first time in a long while – very well.

I was a student by day, PI by night and I loved college. I wrote essays and exams on all the standard sociological subjects and I became familiar with the most famous theorists and philosophers, like Freud and Edmund Burke. At Trinity I also met Pat Byrne, who went on to be a social worker herself and has remained my friend to this day.

To help make ends meet, Evelyn worked part-time at Gaj's restaurant in Baggot Street, which was a great meeting place for lefties, artists, criminals, journalists, politicians, prostitutes and people like me who enjoyed the mix. Margaret Gaj was the owner and she ran her restaurant against all the standard, sacred rules – most important, to Margaret, the customer was usually wrong. A large woman who favoured black clothes and could be as intimidating as any man, she had her own lunchtime table for her favourite people, who included me, Doctor Noël Browne, a prostitute named Lyn Madden, two bank robbers, Brigid Barry, whom I had met when we were both social workers and who was by then a barrister, and to round things out, a member of the aristocracy, Lady Christine Longford.

I felt completely at home in the atmosphere, stories and aggro of Gaj's and it was a hugely popular place. The small vases of fresh flowers were one small delicacy on the plain wooden tables. Fancy restaurants today would call Gaj's furniture 'rustic', but back then, it was just comfortable. The chefs would know to leave the first-floor kitchen windows open in case any patron had to run through in a hurry and jump out on to the roof of the neighbouring building. I preferred to sit where I could put my back right up against the wall and observe the clientèle, free from the worry that someone could catch me off-guard from behind.

I found an unlikely mirror image of myself in Margaret. She was the kind of woman who was known to have groups of travellers in to the restaurant for a meal, free of charge, between the lunch and dinner hours, or to make great vats of hot soup on winter nights for the prostitutes who worked down at the canal nearby. She would visit the district court weekly, usually on a Monday, and shout instructions to the defendants as they were brought into the courtroom to plead not guilty and avail of all their rights. The Gardaí thought she was a nuisance but one of the judges would nod at her and say calmly, 'Good morning, Margaret,' with a quiet sort of respect. Margaret was hugely charitable to people in need at a time when there weren't that many other places they could turn to for help; the many charities and homeless centres that are scattered throughout the city today were yet to be established. Physically, we couldn't have been more different. I was ridiculously small; Margaret was uncommonly large. But we shared an innate empathy for the underdog. We formed a bond of friendship based on good works, a mutual love of the aggro that took place daily in Gaj's and a compulsion to see justice, or at least its closet possible approximation, done as often as possible.

When the two of us sit at a table together nowadays, Margaret, now aged ninety-two and I in my seventies, the years fall away and I'm told we look downright conspiratorial. We're old friends with some secrets and scores of shared stories and memories.

'Remember the guy, Margaret, what was his name, who used to come in to the restaurant who was a warlock? That's what they call a male witch, isn't it? The guy with the keys hanging around his neck…' I start.

Margaret knows who I'm talking about but she can't remember his name. Outsiders listening in on this conversation might be tempted to scoff at the mention of a warlock with a necklace of keys but it's true and this guy was really a character. There's more than a little of the whimsical in our encounters these days.

Our joint memories also conjure another vaguely mystical image of a figure I remember only as 'the Egyptian'. Another regular at Gaj's, the Egyptian was a friendly young man who had come to Ireland after dropping out of medical school at home for lack of funds. Anyone who spent any length of time talking to him could tell he was very intelligent and Gaj's customers began calling in specifically to seek out the Egyptian for medical advice for their health problems. He was cheaper than a visit to the doctor and he was often easier to access.

I like to get Margaret talking about old poker games. She was an excellent poker player and in the days before women's lib and even thereafter, she benefited from many a man's misguided notion that women simply could not play cards. Margaret played occasionally in her own house, at the Poker Classics games and in GAA clubs. Some games were played only with fake money, which I've always maintained is pointless. If you're going to play poker, you play for real money or not at all. Margaret feels the same. One night she started a 'friendly game' with another woman for real notes off to the side and a man who had just received his week's pay and was feeling foolishly confident fell right into her trap. In a rush of sympathy, I tried to warn him that he didn't know with whom he was dealing; with Margaret, there wasn't any such thing as a 'friendly game'. He went ahead and she cleaned him out. Although he left with empty pockets, at least he was armed with experience's lesson: never pick a woman as an easy mark based on her gender alone.

Margaret was infinitely moderate and controlled in her card playing and she also liked to do a little gambling of sorts with customers in her restaurant when it came time to pay the bill. She had a system she called 'double or quits': customers had the option to pay the regular listed price for their meals, or they could take a chance and flip Margaret for their bill. If the customer won, he got his meal free but if Margaret won, the customer paid double. She figured that the laws of averages would work out in her favour and to the best of her knowledge, they did.

Margaret is also the only person I've ever met who has been escorted on the arm of a Garda inspector to the Garda station after arrest. The Gardaí got her one day along with a crowd of others for leafleting (most likely for the Prisoner's Rights Organisation, with which Margaret was very involved). When one young Garda attempted to guide her into the back of the transport vehicle, which stood high off the ground, she told him in no uncertain terms that she couldn't get into it because of her bad leg. She wasn't exaggerating just to be difficult, either, or to avoid arrest. The young Garda stood dumbfounded. Now what to do? An older Garda, an inspector who knew Margaret, came over to her rather grandly and said, 'Margaret, I will escort you to the station,' and offered her his arm. They walked like that, like a lady and a gentleman, down the street to the Bridewell.

There's a photograph of Margaret when she was very young, smiling like she's having the day of her life, on a hill, probably in her native Scotland. Her hair is blowing around and she's hiking up her skirt comically for the camera but she still appears ultimately modest. 'Look at you, Margaret,' I say. 'That was really risqué in those days.' People have asked us about the circumstances of our first meeting but we're both stumped. It had to be in the restaurant but we can't remember when or how. We just always seem to have known one another.

At the close of my year at Trinity, I realised I couldn't really afford to be a student by day and a PI by night for as long as it would take to earn my degree. I was sorry to have to leave college but by now I was used to completely changing direction every few years. Whatever I ended up doing, I hoped it wouldn't take me so far so that I couldn't stop in to Gaj's for my regular lunch.

9

The Fixer

You can take the boy out of Kilfenora but you can't take Kilfenora out of the boy. I know I'll always be one of those people who have unbreakable ties to the place where I grew up. It's hard to explain but I feel a similarly strong connection to social work. I feel as if I'll always be a social worker in my own way, even though I haven't held that title in decades.

A few weeks after the ISPCC sacked me, a social worker friend of mine called me with a problem. She worked for an organisation called Cherish, which was founded for the support of single mothers who wanted to keep and raise their children. There was a young single mother who was in a wheelchair and who had just had a baby girl at a home for unmarried mothers on the Navan Road that was run by nuns. She was a very accomplished seamstress, which is how she earned her living, and she had a ground-floor flat of her own in Glenageary, near Dún Laoghaire. After she had given birth to her daughter, she asked to breastfeed her. The nuns wouldn't let her, nor would they let her touch her baby. When she was ready to leave and take the baby with her, they refused to give it to her. In desperation, she went to the children's section of the Eastern Health Board (EHB) and was referred to a social worker there, who referred the case to a senior official. He told the social worker to drop the matter entirely.

Frantic, the young mother went to Cherish, who she had heard might be able to help her, and my friend there was assigned to her case. Things got complicated for her very quickly. She could see that there was no reason why the young mother shouldn't be allowed to keep her baby – she was capable and independent and her being in a wheelchair was no barrier to her raising her own child. But the EHB official knew that the mother was taking her case to Cherish and threatened the organisation that its annual grant from the health board would be withheld the following year if the matter wasn't dropped immediately. Without this grant, Cherish wouldn't have been able to operate.

My friend at Cherish was terribly caught but she hoped I might be able to help. For one thing, I wasn't beholden to the ISPCC any more, having just been sacked, but I knew the right people to talk to and would be determined enough to get a good result, if it was at all possible, for the young mother. I rang the EHB official and told him he had twenty-four hours to give the baby back to the mother.

The first thing the EHB official did was to ring the ISPCC, my former employers, with threats on the tip of his tongue. To his shock, he found out they had absolutely no control over me any more. He knew I would be much harder to deal with as a rogue entity, which is what I really was anyway, even when I was on the ISPCC payroll. Realising he couldn't intimidate or threaten me into dropping the case, the EHB official rang me to say that the health board would hold a 'case conference' on the young mother's situation. I assumed she and I, as her representative, would be invited, or at least allowed to attend, but he said no.

'Right, see you in court,' I said. I immediately went to a firm of solicitors and they took on yet another pro bono case. They issued habeas corpus proceedings in the High Court against the EHB official and the two nuns in charge at Navan Road. Adrian Hardiman, a young junior counsel at the time, who now sits on the Supreme Court, handled the brief. The judge read the affidavits and asked the defendants if there was any indication that the young mother had abandoned her baby. The representatives from the health board and the nuns said, 'No but…' But the judge wouldn't let them finish. 'But nothing,' he said. He ordered them to give the baby back to her mother at half-past two that afternoon.

I went to the home on the Navan Road with the mother to collect her baby. The nuns were so rude that they were only short of throwing the baby at us. A few years later, I saw the mother in a supermarket in Baggot Street with a little girl running alongside her, throwing things into her shopping basket.

There were whispers among my old colleagues that I had taken charge of that case and found the solicitors to represent the mother as vengeance against the health board, which was closely linked to the ISPCC. But I was never paid a penny for my involvement in the case and for me it was a simple case of the authorities trying, openly and arrogantly, to kidnap the baby of a competent woman. There was no way that was going to happen if I could help it and it had nothing to do with revenge.

I had my own battles to fight in those days. There was a short period between the time I was sacked by the ISPCC and when I decided to go to Trinity and become a PI when I was completely unemployed and I signed on to get unemployment benefit from the department of social welfare. I drew my money the first week with no problem but when I went to the office the second week I was told to see the supervisor, who very politely told me I had been disallowed. Someone had seen me driving a red lorry during the day and had reported me to the office, which meant I had made myself unavailable for work – grounds for blocking my welfare money. I asked to have the reason in writing. The supervisor was extremely courteous and also told me I could appeal the decision.

With the reason for my disallowance in writing and the appeal form in hand, I went straight over to government publications, bought a copy of the 1964 Social Welfare Act and read section 15, the one that applied to my situation. I made up my mind that there were fundamental flaws in the legislation. First of all, it granted judicial powers to a deciding officer which should have been reserved for a judge in a courtroom. Secondly, I had been given no chance to defend myself or explain offending actions before they stopped my money.

I decided it was against the rules of natural justice. So I ran over to the Law Library and got a junior counsel and we drafted an affidavit and applied for an order of certiorari against the Minister for Social Welfare and the Attorney General, to quash the decision of the deciding officer. Far from being intimidated by paperwork and legalese, I thrive on such intricacies. It was an interesting challenge. In a way, it reminded me of the nasty Christian Brother in Synge Street asking what could they expect of a boy from Kimmage – the bully picking on the vulnerable.

I had been disallowed my payment on a Friday and was in court the following Monday. The High Court granted a conditional order of certiorari, which gave the state ten days to defend its decision to stop my labour money. Copies of the order had to be served on the manager at the labour exchange, the Department of Social Welfare and the State Solicitor's office. I drafted all those up in a hurry and ran around serving them myself. I was, after all, unemployed, so I had the time.

When I served the manager at the labour exchange, he was quite upset; such a thing had probably never happened to him before. The Secretary of the Department of Social Welfare was cooler and very courteous. He had an assistant go off and make an extra photocopy of the original brief while he skimmed his own copy and I waited.

'Does this man not know that the decision of the deciding officer is final?' he asked me, not realising that I was the man in question.

'Yes, but he mightn't agree,' I said.

'Well, he must have plenty of money,' he said.

'Well, I don't, actually,' I said. The Secretary was quite embarrassed.

I did well in the courts not only because paperwork didn't intimidate me but because I knew which barristers to get for which specific areas of law. In this case, my solicitors briefed Ercus Stewart, who was then a junior counsel and is now an eminent senior counsel in the area of labour law. Ruairi O'Hanlon acted as my senior counsel and he was so good that the state tried to get him to represent it after I had already confirmed that he would act for me. The senior counsel on the other side discussed the case with O'Hanlon, Stewart and the solicitors and they agreed that I had the state by the short and curlies. The section of the act in question was against natural justice and if I pushed it, it would fall. The state's senior counsel told me and my solicitors that if we came into court within the next few days, the state would concede, pay my costs and I would get my money.

'Mr Crummey, if you go over to the labour exchange now, they will have your money waiting for you,' the state's senior counsel told me as we left the court.

'No, he can't collect it now; he has to go somewhere in the red lorry first!' Ercus Stewart replied, laughing. What I had actually been dòing in the red lorry was a favour for a friend whose wife had just died, driving the lorry from A to B. As for who reported me, I don't know who it was and never will. I think of the number of other applicants who had their money stopped against natural justice and who just didn't know how to say, 'Well, I'll have a go at this,' and would therefore not have got their money. That's the important thing and a shame.

After my year at Trinity I spent another few years as a PI but for much of that time I was thinking about what my next job was going to be. My friend Syl Collins had helped me with the dangerous, rogue security side of my social work; now maybe I could work with Syl at the building trade. When you need work, you do anything that comes your way. He would have jobs going and I'd say, 'Any chance of labouring on the building with you?' Syl was a foreman on building sites and I was fairly sure I could learn about the construction trade alongside my friend.

I was a crazy builder. I knew fuck all about it but I didn't let on that I didn't. And I had good foremen.

After a few years labouring on sites from the tail end of the 1970s through the early 1980s, I set up my own building company and I used the same men on my jobs I had worked with and got to know through working with Syl. Syl's nephew, the plumber Patrick O'Dowd, was one of my favourites. When I first started working with him, he always brought a big cape and ensconced himself under it. I asked him why. 'Because, I know you and I know you're watching me,' Patrick said. 'And if you learn how to do this, you won't be calling me any more – you'll just do it yourself!'

Few men working on the buildings guarded their trade secrets as closely as Patrick the plumber did at the beginning but I knew many of them thought I was, in their kindest estimation of me, unorthodox. One of the indelible experiences that would have given them that impression included the day when I showed up for work with knitting needles, wool and a work-in-progress. The crew didn't know what to make of me when I produced my needlework at lunchtime in front of all of them – hard men, every one. My attitude was that if they didn't like it, they knew what to do. I was making vests for the charities to send to Ethiopia. I've always enjoyed knitting and didn't see any reason why I should hesitate to do it on a building site. My co-workers may have been bemused but they may also have felt a twinge of admiration for the knitting builder who would obviously do what he liked regardless of other people's opinions.

I won them over, which was proven when I needed them to

help me with a favour for a good friend. Brigid Barry, my former colleague from the ISPCC, was now a barrister. Her husband Oliver was a very successful engineer who had made most of his money on big projects in Saudi Arabia. But friends of his in the industry encouraged him not to put all his eggs in one basket and to start bulking up on the Irish side of his business. He took their advice and opened up his own factory in Walkinstown. He was getting a good number of contracts in Ireland and was undertaking fewer projects in Saudi Arabia; he was also saving himself travel costs and stress by not having to fly over so often. But when the worst effects of Ireland's economic collapse in the 1980s began to hit Oliver's business and Ireland was haemorrhaging emigrants desperate for work, he found himself in a bind. The only way he could recover was if he could build his business in Saudi Arabia back up to where it was before.

Oliver had to make his situation sound a little better and more confidence-inspiring than it actually was in order to secure Saudi contracts. Tumbleweeds would have rolled freely through his big Walkinstown factory, which now had a secretary in it and not a single other worker, for the simple reason that there was no work to be had. The Saudis may have got a little suspicious as to why Oliver's business seemed to be immune to the disaster the rest of Ireland was experiencing. They rang him up one night to tell him that they would be arriving in Shannon airport the next day to see his factory and they would appreciate it if he could pick them up, drive them back to Dublin and give them a tour.

Oliver put down the phone with a heavy, sinking, horrible feeling and told Brigid he was finished, ruined, heading for bankruptcy. Brigid thought for a minute and said, 'Don't do anything until I ring Frank Crummey.' Oliver was confused. 'Brigid, what does Frank Crummey have to do with this?' he asked.

'Oliver, I'm just telling you,' she said, and her tone was confidence itself.

Brigid rang me and told me the story. I said that she should tell Oliver to go out to Shannon and pick up the Saudis and play it by ear when he arrived at the factory with them.

So down to Shannon goes Oliver in his big car. I collected the keys, went into the factory and told the secretary there to play along with me, too, when Oliver arrived. I had filled all my mates from the building site in on the plan and they came straight to the factory that morning to pose as the workers. Now I had the men to make it look like a working factory but I didn't have any materials. Since Oliver hadn't been filling any orders, there wasn't much for the men to pretend they were working on in the factory. With the bits and pieces they did have to work with, I directed one man to weld, another to hammer and so forth, generally making noise and looking busy – but not until we heard Oliver's car coming up the road. There was no use in wasting everyone's energy.

When Oliver walked in with the businessmen in tow, I went up to him immediately.

'Excuse me, Mr Barry, may I interrupt you?' I said. 'That order's gone out. We're just sweeping up now for that material we have ordered for the day after tomorrow. I have the lads doing…'

'Thank you very much,' Oliver said hastily. The Saudis took a quick look around at all the men working and then went up to Oliver's office with him. After they emerged and Oliver had left with them in his car, the secretary came back to me with a fistful of money and said that Mr Barry had told her to give it to me to take my mates to the pub to get drunk. We all went down to the nearby Kestrel pub and the men had only started in on their first lovely pints when the young secretary came bursting in, panicked.

'They're coming back!' she said.

Everyone ran back up the road, taking up their stations again just in time. Oliver got the contract and saved his business. My friends eventually got back to their pints. Later, Oliver asked

Brigid how in the name of God she had known that I was the man to ring in search of a solution.

'Because,' she said matter-of-factly, 'he's a fixer.'

I wasn't done helping Oliver yet. A few years later, while still a young man, Oliver fell seriously ill with cancer. For a while he felt it was necessary to conceal the gravity of his illness from his clients. On one of the Saudis' visits this time, when Oliver wasn't well enough to drive, I went along with him to the airport as his 'chauffeur'.

After a few years in the building trade, I began to pick things up and, as you do with most jobs, I learned its intricacies and nuances much better. I became especially good at installing sewers and put in the whole sewer system free of charge for the Shanty, a women's resource centre in west Tallaght for which two women donated a plot of their land. Several other skilled labourers had donated their time to help built the centre and Mary Robinson did the opening.

The worst sewer job I ever worked on was for a Raheny butcher. One day, the butcher walked into his shop and was overwhelmed by the smell of sewage. Upon inspection he discovered that a pipe had burst and sewage was backing up through one of the drains in the floor of his back room. He called in Syl Collins, his cousin, to have a look. I realised that it would take several days to fix the cracked sewer, which meant closing the shop for the duration. The butcher was upset by the idea; he literally couldn't afford to do this. Wasn't there another option for fixing the pipe that would allow him to stay open? I saw that it could be repaired from underneath instead of from above. This would require a lot of extra labour for the digging and it would take much longer but it would allow him to stay open for business. The butcher told me it didn't matter about the cost; it would still be worth it for him to stay open.

Even though I was covered from head to foot in oilskins, when

I emerged from underneath the gushing sewage, no hose had enough water to really clean me: the stench was in my nose for days. But the butcher's shop was saved and its owner grateful.

That was my dirtiest job but there were others that turned out to be more dangerous. I did my fair share of house demolitions and there was one house in Sandymount that was in such bad condition that one of the upper floors literally collapsed under my feet. I felt it move right before it gave way and made a swift half-leap, half-grab for the fireplace built into the wall. I hung there while the men working with me (miraculously, no one was hurt) rushed around to set the ladder up and get me down. Still suspended, I heard the floor collapse on to the floor below and then crash right down to the ground.

The walls of the house were still intact, so once I had disentangled myself from the fireplace and got outside, I spotted what I thought was the keystone keeping everything standing. So we got the ropes and the men and we heaved. When I think of it now, I realise how unsafe it was. We didn't have hard hats or anything like it then but sure, what were we to do? We needed the money.

After the ISPCC sacked me I had helped some other people, free of charge, besides the young mother who almost lost her baby. Margaret Gaj liked putting me up to wild things. She was always ringing me. 'C'mon, we have something to do,' she'd say. And we did totally mad things, we did. Margaret had no fear and I admired that. I remember how she would deliberately wind customers up in her restaurant instead of trying to calm them, knowing they'd probably throw a chair or table at her in frustration. I think she enjoyed it. It would be a great bit of aggro for the night.

Sometimes, especially during my years as a PI, I would serve summonses for a little extra money and Margaret would go along as my getaway driver. We served a summons once on a car mechanic working in Clanbrassil Street. I went inside with the document while Margaret waited behind the wheel. I asked one of the first men I saw in the place to identify my man, since I had no idea what he looked like. He pointed out a man with his back to us, leaning over a car engine. Caught totally unawares, he was none too pleased at the appearance of an impish little man clutching his summons and saying, 'You've been identified and I'm serving this.' He took a swing at me and I did the sensible thing and ran for the car. Only there was no use getting into the car, because he would have got in behind me and I'd have been battered. So I swung left, down to Leonard's Corner, with Margaret driving slowly alongside us as I ran.

I turned up on to the South Circular Road with the mechanic still after me. But I was a marathon man. I knew I'd prevail. Just like I knew being small and unthreatening had saved me in the past because people hesitated to beat up a little guy, being small and fit would save me now. He had no chance of catching me but I let him run to try. If I had tripped, I'd have been in shit. When I got round to South Circular Road and I could hear him straining for breath, I said, 'Gotcha just the same. You've been served. See you in court on Tuesday.'

I ended up giving evidence in court on the serving of the summons and I told the judge how the mechanic had punched me.

'And then what did you do, Mr Crummey?' the judge asked.

'I ran, my Lord, I ran,' I said.

'Very prudent,' the judge remarked.

Another time, I was serving a summons on my own to a corporation house out in Coolock. When I rang the bell, the front door opened and a horse walked out past me and into the front garden. And then behind the horse was some young one who said, 'Yeah, what do you want?' No, 'Excuse the horse,' or anything. The house had a parlour, a kitchen and two bedrooms upstairs. Where had the horse been?

On one of the coldest nights in many winters in the mid-1970s, Margaret rang me and asked what I was doing. I told her nothing much – it was fairly late and I was just relaxing at home. She had just made a big pot of soup in her house in Pembroke Lane and asked if I would go down to the canal to see if any of the prostitutes wanted to come up for a bowl. When I got down to the canal, there was only one girl working and I didn't recognise her although I would have known most of the girls there from acting as Margaret's messenger many times before, or seeing them in the restaurant. She assumed I was a customer until I told her why I was there and invited her to Margaret's.

She was frozen. And I mean frozen. She got into my car and we drove back to Margaret's, where we gave her a bowl of hot lovely soup. She was still so cold that we washed her feet and legs in warm water to help her get some heat back. She spoke with an English accent and it was easy to see she was not like most of the other prostitutes. She was both extremely articulate and well-read, which I admit, I hope without judgement, was a not common among the types who usually worked the canal. Eventually we asked her why she was the only one out that night when all the others had decided it was much too cold and she told us that her pimp lived in England but was paying a Donnybrook Garda to keep an eye on her. If she wasn't out working, he would hear about it and she'd be beaten. Her name was Lyn Madden.

Looking back on it, I think my involvement with the pimps for whom Lyn worked is in the running for one of the most naïve things I've ever done. I thought it was particularly disgraceful that Lyn's pimp was living in England, from where he couldn't even offer her any protection, but was siphoning about £600 per week from her earnings. In a moment of madness, I asked Lyn if she'd give her money to me instead and I'd put it in the building society for her. And didn't she agree!

Her pimp was not impressed. Unimpressed is an under-statement – in fact, he was livid. He decided to find out more about this 'little weasel' – his eventual nickname for me – who was interfering with his source of income. Unfortunately, Lyn's relationship with the pimp, Craig Nelson, was more than just business-based as she had three children with him. When he began phoning Lyn and demanding to talk to me, I took one of his outraged phone calls.

I told him to go to hell, that he wasn't getting any more money and he could do what he liked. But what he liked included harassing me and my family at home and threatening to kill me. He rang the house constantly and my children would often answer and speak Irish to him before laughing and hanging up. 'It's just Craig Nelson,' they'd say. When he flew over to Dublin from England, though, it became less of a game.

One day my daughter, Edel, was playing in the front garden with the neighbourhood children when a car pulled up across the street. A man got out and came over to the children. 'Can anyone tell me if Mr Crummey's little girl is out today?' he asked politely in a strong British accent. A clever girl in the group who knew Edel well, a child of only nine or ten years old, answered immediately, 'She's not well, she's sick in bed,' at which he walked back to his car and drove away. The girl grabbed Edel's arm and walked her straight to her own house – it was during the time when Evelyn was waitressing at Gaj's and she wasn't home yet – where she told her mother that a man with an English accent had been asking after Edel. Since everyone on the street knew about my trouble with Nelson, the girl had figured out that an English man looking for one of the Crummey children was a bad sign.

Around the same time, Evelyn and I were going through the day's post. Evelyn opened a large, oddly lumpy envelope and heard a tinny, clinking sound. Four bullets had fallen out on to the floor. She turned to me and, practical as always, said, 'Those must be for you. Nobody would want to kill me.'

At around two o'clock on the morning after the day the Pope

said Mass in the Phoenix Park on his famous visit to Ireland in September 1979, the family woke up to the echoing sound of shattering glass all over the house. Every one of our front windows had been smashed and a gleaming spanner was lodged in one of the frames. No one was hurt but we knew the trouble that had started off with harassing phone calls was getting much more serious now. The Kilfenora neighbours came forth to help us board up our windows in the middle of the night, slagging me the whole time. 'When are you going to move off this street and finally give us some peace?' they said. One of them asked, seriously, if he could keep the spanner. It looked nice, new and useful.

Eventually, Craig Nelson was arrested and I visited him in Mountjoy. I brought along my friend Pat Byrne, whom I'd met at Trinity. Pat had lived a refined, sheltered and financially comfortable life. She was shocked and bewildered upon meeting the pimp. I confronted him with the accusation that during one of his beatings of Lyn, he had fractured her skull. Nelson fired back with what he probably thought was a clever rejoinder. 'No, I didn't. I punched her in the face and she fractured her skull when she hit the ground.'

The Kilfenora neighbours hadn't really wanted me to move (well, I'm sure a few did but not the majority) but that's what ended up happening. Nelson wouldn't always be in jail and he had dangerous friends who knew where I lived. We moved to a lovely, big house in Knockair but I was heartbroken to have to sell my mother's house, on the street where I still knew every family name and faces to correspond to every house number. It was a life transition that had a finality to it unlike any other, including my travels to Australia and London. On both these occasions, I had planned on coming home to Dublin and settling back on Kilfenora. I stilled visit the old road all the time but I would never live there again. Many people arrive at the realisation that the house they grew up in is no longer their home when they

Frank's First Holy Communion, 1979. From left: Elizabeth, Evelyn, Frank, Edel, myself, Jane, my mother and Deirdre.

Syl Collins, my back-up when there was trouble, speaking at my seventieth birthday party in July 2006.

Posters erected by my pro-life opponents, 1997.

From left: my son, Frank, my wife Evelyn, Margaret Gaj and my daughter Elizabeth in 2006.

Dubliner of the Month
APRIL '92

Frank Crummey

I am awarded Dubliner of the Month in April 1992.
From left: Dermot Lacey, myself and Denis O'Brien.

Above left: A function for Women's Refuge in Rathmines. From left: Kathy Moore, manager of the Refuge, President Mary McAleese and I.

Left: The opening of the new Marie Stopes International Clinic in Berkeley Road, 2005. From left: Myself, Doreen McCarthy and Nell McCafferty.

Above: Women's Refuge presents me with a statuette. From left: Kathy Moore, manager, myself, my wife, Evelyn, and Lorraine Donoghue

A poster on display in Women's Refuge to record my life.

*Judge Peter Smithwick and I celebrating the twenty-first
birthday of the Irish Institute of Legal Executives.*

My ten grandchildren. Front row, from left: Grace, Liam, Peter, Emer and Aidan.
Middle row, from left: Sean and Rachel.
Back row, from left: Conor, Kevin and Fiona.

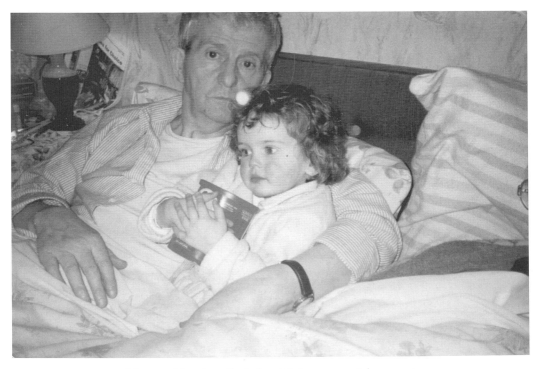

My granddaughter Rachel and I share a special moment.

finish college or get their first job and move out on their own. For me, it came much later than that, when I was already married and had five children. But my age didn't make it any easier – in fact, it was probably much harder to leave the road where all the scenes not only of my own childhood but a good chunk of my children's childhood had played out. But it made the move much easier that I knew I'd be back on the old road to drop into the neighbours nearly every day.

Nelson left the country, which marked the end of the relationship between him and Lyn, but she got involved with another violent man who, like Nelson, spent her earnings from working on the streets, beat her and eventually attacked her with a knife, slashing her face. It was while she was recovering in hospital that she met one of her friend's pimps, John Cullen. That's when her nightmare really began.

Cullen was recognised even in Dublin's subculture as an extremely unpredictable, unstable and dangerous man. Nelson had fractured her skull; Cullen was more cruelly creative in his revenge. He was no stranger to the courtroom and had been brought up on assault and other charges numerous times. One of the women who had testified against him before and who had been a friend and flatmate of Lyn's was Dolores Lynch. Dolores had worked as a prostitute with Lyn and she knew exactly how dangerous Cullen was. While he was in jail, she was very careful about concealing her whereabouts in Dublin but he was obsessed with getting revenge on her for her testimony against him.

Dolores had left prostitution and was working as a hospital attendant, living quietly in a house near the city centre with her mother and aunt, when Cullen finally did find her and set the fire in her house that killed all three women. Lyn had been with him that night while he committed the crime but testified in court that she knew nothing about where they were going or what he was doing until it was too late. Such was her fear of Cullen and his complete domination of her, that when he told her to get into the car with him around 3am on the morning of the murder, 16 January 1983, she did as she was told. He brought a bag with him which he opened outside what Lyn later found out was Dolores's house. It contained several knives, a hammer, two containers full of petrol, firelighters and matches. He found an open window, delighted he didn't even have to pry one open or break one, lit the devices and placed them carefully inside the room.

Lyn heard screams and the sound of glass shattering as she and Cullen ran away. Back at her flat, he systematically disposed of their clothing and the contents of his bag. Lyn didn't know whose house it was that Cullen had set fire to until she watched the nine o'clock news that night. When she found out that Dolores had died along with her mother and aunt, she was devastated. The murders made her realise, after all the abuse she had endured at Cullen's hands, just how much damage, destruction and brutality he was capable of. She testified against Cullen at his murder trial, wrote her book with Levine and eventually moved back to England. No one from her regular Gaj's lunch table has seen her or been able to contact her in years but Margaret Gaj receives a Christmas card, without a return address, every single year.

One of the things I loved most about Margaret Gaj and her treatment of Lyn, as well as the other prostitutes along the canal, was that she was happy to help them without trying to save their eternal souls. So was I. Catholic organisations like the Legion of Mary had their place but conversion was usually a lurking condition of their assistance. Margaret and I knew that sometimes the best thing we could do for someone was to give her a meal and talk to her. Within the world we were trying so hard to change, we knew that most individuals changed very little themselves. I found Lyn a lovely woman from the first freezing night I met her on her own down at the canal but I knew that her flaw was her attraction to vicious men – her inability to occupy any role other than that of a victim. There was nothing I, Margaret, or anyone else could do to help her break out of that cycle until she decided to do it herself.

I knew just how deeply some people's flaws were ingrained from my years in social work. There was one woman I had tried to help, a serial shoplifter, who illustrated the point. She had been in and out of the courts so many times that the judge had finally had enough. 'I don't care if you have young children or not, if you come before me again, you're going inside,' she told the woman. About a month later, the shoplifter appeared in court again for the same offences and her solicitor had told her this was the time she was definitely going to jail. She asked me to make an appeal to the judge for her, so I went in and told the judge that she really had changed and I had just helped her find a job making rosary beads, so she wouldn't have any need to shoplift any longer. My story was true. 'I'm not asking you, I'm begging you, give her one more chance,' I said to the judge.

The judge read the woman the riot act and told her that she was still tempted to send her to jail. But, seeing as I had made such an appeal on her behalf and that she had a job making rosary beads now, she said she would give her one more chance. The shoplifter was naturally delighted and she told me that she could never repay me but that I should come around to her house, which was right around the corner, for a cup of tea. I was having tea with her when she said, 'I really can never repay you but what size shirt do you wear?'

'Fourteen and a half,' I said.

'Great, I'll nick a few for you tomorrow,' she said.

Margaret and I were happy to help people in whatever ways we could, learning not to expect complete transformations. But Margaret also thought it was important for Dubliners to get a glimpse into what the prostitutes' lives were like. To many in the city, women like Lyn were part of an invisible subculture far beneath the surface of society. One young journalist who frequented Gaj's came into the restaurant one day, upset because she had just come from the canal where she had tried to interview some of the girls. They had threatened to throw her into the water. Margaret asked me to bring the journalist back down to the canal and vouch for her. When they arrived, the prostitutes, recognising me, came over to my car to say hello. Once they knew she was with me, they gave the journalist a terrific interview. But I noticed that one of them kept her distance. 'It's all right, it's just Crummey,' one of the other women told her. But she knew me and she was embarrassed. She was a neighbour's child from Kilfenora.

During my building years, in the early 1980s, the vehicle I was most often seen driving around Dublin in was my beat-up, rusty, Toyota Hiace van. Its size was its best asset and it didn't owe me anything. Friends of mine in the same business knew they could borrow it at a pinch. Another of my acquaintances, the plumber Patrick O'Dowd, whom I'd first met through Syl Collins, borrowed it one day to do a nixer and brought it back to me with exciting news.

'I was driving around and a woman stopped me to say she wanted to use your van in a film,' Patrick said.

I knew most of Syl's friends were messers just like Syl and me. I took the phone number that Patrick handed me without much comment. I wasn't going to ring it until he was gone, in case it was Dublin Zoo or something and then I certainly would never tell him I rang it. I was more than a little surprised when the woman at the other end of the line confirmed that she wanted my van for a film being shot in Dublin and arranged for me to bring it to the location.

The film, directed by Neil Jordan, was *Cal*, a story about the IRA and the Northern Troubles. When I arrived in my van, they were thrilled. Every time they'd tried to rent a Toyota Hiace, they'd always been provided with a shiny new one, when what they actually wanted was one that looked worn, just like mine.

I was in for another surprise. It turned out that neither of the two actors who were supposed to have scenes driving around in the van could actually drive, so as well as renting my van, they asked me to act as a sort of stunt driver, too (although the actual 'stunts' included no more than taking a corner a little on the fast side). Then during the final editing, my driving scenes would be spliced with shots of the actors getting in and out of the van to make it look as if they were driving the whole time.

I enjoyed myself immensely. For starters, the pay was a fabulous £100 pounds a day for sixteen days of work, which meant a great deal to me financially at the time. The catered food was also amazing, so much so that I was greatly tempted to fill my pockets. But what I really loved was talking to the people on the set. I found one of the actors, Ray McAnally, who also appeared in *My Left Foot* with Daniel Day-Lewis, fascinating. He loved telling stories about different characters he'd played and other actors he'd met and he was extremely friendly. I was always amazed at the way he could snap himself back into his character in *Cal* – an unpleasant Orangeman – at a few moments' notice. His whole face would change and he would look really frightening all of a sudden.

Aside from all the perks, my work on the film allowed me to add yet another kind of work to my growing list of jobs, which I always enjoyed. It didn't matter if I was laying sewers or working in the Mansion House: an honest day's work is an honest day's work. It makes no difference to me. Still, I had to admit that my brief stint in the film industry was a nice change from the building sites for a few weeks. Years later, one of my grandsons worked with Neil Jordan on the 2005 film *Breakfast on Pluto*, appearing as the younger version of the main character, a transvestite played by Cillian Murphy. I was delighted that it was a film that highlighted both the hypocrisy and compassion of the Catholic Church in the person of a single character, a priest played by Liam Neeson. It hadn't been necessary for one of my ten grandchildren to appear on the silver screen for me to swell with grandfatherly pride; I had experienced plenty of that with each of them already, but excitement still rippled through the family on the day of the film's première. It was nice to know that Crummey talents were being properly recognised in the younger generation.

I was doing building work one summer in the early 1980s for one of the solicitors I knew well when there was uproar in the office. It was a small firm with only a few solicitors and they had all somehow managed to schedule their holidays for the same two weeks. If one of them didn't cancel or reschedule his plans, they'd have to close the office.

The firm, Coughlan and McNally, had rented a former ladies' hairdressing salon in which to set up shop about a year earlier and I was the builder who had converted it for them. I took out all the sinks and hairdressing equipment and changed it into proper offices. I was back in the summer of disastrous schedules fixing a sewer pipe when I heard the furore over conflicting plans and thought I might be of service. Social work, family planning, Reform, my own labour case and serving summonses had all taught me enough about the courts for me to feel comfortable with basic legal terms and documents. Paul McNally offered me a very small office at the back of their building, not much bigger than a closet, and I switched immediately from conveyancing to family law. I set to work, going directly from overalls to suit.

10

THE REFUGE

Kathy Moore started working as an assistant at the women's refuge in Rathmines soon after it opened more than twenty years ago. Today, she's the manager. People might think that Kathy has seen it all by now and isn't surprised by the stories of the abused women and children who stream through the doors of the refuge but she would never say that herself. People's capacity for cruelty will never cease to amaze her. Kathy and I have known each other for years and have seen a lot of savagery together. We've helped each other to deal with it through a shared sense of dark humour that not everyone would understand or approve of. I have great respect for the way Kathy Moore and her assistant manager, Lorraine Donoghue, take care of the women in the refuge.

Kathy could tell you stories about the woman who was born on the steps of a bank and who had been sexually abused from the age of two by an elder brother. She came to the refuge one night in a wedding dress soaked in blood, spent years in and out of one violent situation after another and finally ended up at the bottom of the canal, a shade past forty years old, unable to bear any longer the burden of her own memories. She could tell you about the woman at the refuge who received an envelope from her estranged husband that contained the chopped-up pieces of her children's pet pigeons. She could tell you about the man who came to the refuge to harass his wife and children and then hid on the altar of the church across the street when Kathy rang the Gardaí to take him away, standing stock-still in an effort to blend in with the statues. She deals with people in desperate situations every day and it's her job to stay calm and as impartial as possible. Some days, it's easier than others.

'When you're working with crisis cases, you have to be very, very careful about what you say,' she says. Kathy also knew and admired Doctor Paddy Leahy and she'll never forget one of his stories that proves the point about being careful what you say. Doctor Leahy saw a woman in his clinic one day whom he regularly treated for the cuts, abrasions and bruises that resulted from her husband's abuse. 'If it were me, I'd slit his throat,' he muttered as he looked after her. The woman went home and about half an hour later, Doctor Leahy was called out to her house. To his horror he found that she had attacked her husband with a knife.

The refuge itself is a plain, nondescript single-level building with large, solid wooden doors. Inside there's an enclosed courtyard with a playground, designed deliberately to discourage the kidnapping of children, which has happened more than once. Children's artwork covers the walls outside a very large common room and kitchen, where many of the women eat together. The same corridor also displays large, glossy photographs of President Mary McAleese's visit to the refuge early in 2006 for its twentieth anniversary, showing smiles all around from Kathy, her staff and me. Down another corridor are most of the rooms that the women and children stay in and there's also a children's playroom that opens out into a generous back garden. The newest addition to the refuge is a lovely, soft-looking 'tranquillity' room decorated in cool purples and blues with candles and plush furniture. It's for the women to use one at a time if they need a few minutes to themselves to relax. Right outside the tranquillity room hangs a recently installed poster-sized collage of photos commemorating my service to the refuge, which has a kind of 'This is your life' look to it. There are photographs of me from primary school to the present. One of the headlines from an old magazine article about me, accompanied by a photograph which is immediately identifiable as having been taken in the 1970s because of the clothing and hairstyle, is eye-catching: 'The Legendary Fighter Who Won't Give Up.' My face looks even thinner than usual and my eyes larger but it is unmistakably me. The publication date across the top reveals that I had just been sacked by the ISPCC.

Most solicitors and legal executives work within an office that has its own secretary. When I began working in Paul McNally's office, it was no different, but I was put on to a fair number of my cases not by the office secretary but by my unofficial switchboard operator and great friend, Margaret Gaj. My becoming a legal executive brought our charitable activities to a whole new level. Now, instead of helping serve the odd summons to an abusive husband to appear in court, I was in court myself, attending barristers acting for the women. I naturally gravitated toward the area of family law; it felt good to be able to help people by getting a good result – and a kind of closure to hard times in their lives – in court.

It was Margaret Gaj who asked me to get involved in my first case for a woman who was staying in the refuge. Someone from the refuge had rung her to ask if she knew anyone who would be interested in the case, because people knew to ring Margaret for things like that. As I began work on the case, which involved a separation between parents of children whose father had habitually sexually abused them, I met at least four more women for whom my office acted, all free of charge.

I have represented some utterly fabulous and unique women over the years, including one of the largest, toughest women I've ever met, who had a deep, gruff voice and used to be put in charge of organising the kitchen clean-up every night because it was guaranteed that none of the other women would give her any hassle. 'If these pots aren't done in five minutes, they're going out the window and you with them,' she used to tell the others. She didn't think I was moving fast enough on one of the particulars of her separation. 'Are you acting for me, or are you only acting?' she asked once when we were discussing the progress of her case. Kathy Moore took her aside later and reminded her, gently enough, that I was working for her for nothing. 'Well, it's not good enough,' she replied, but she may have been as shamed as it was possible for her to be, because she slightly softened her demands.

Other women were tough, too, in ways that could be funny, although this kind of humour was grounded in years of tragedy. I sat out in the enclosed playground one afternoon with another refuge staffer to hear a mother shout to her small daughter, 'Vic-fucking-toria, get in here right now!' She was so used to punctuating everything with the expletive that she couldn't stop herself even with her own daughter's name. After my friend and I were through laughing, I said seriously, 'The teacher in school is going to ask her what her name is and she'll say, 'Vic-fucking-toria...'

There are three women I acted for who were, in their own words, 'inmates' together at the refuge – Mary, Sheila and Anne. More than twenty years after I first met them all and represented them in court, helping them leave behind the worst nightmares of their lives – their abusive husbands – they still get together every Christmas and take me out to one of Dublin's fancy restaurants for dinner. I always get a variation of the same gift – a new shirt, tie and jumper, my regular working uniform for the courts, worn under a somewhat rumpled suit jacket and with matching trousers.

Mary, Sheila and Anne all remember the exact dates they entered the refuge, within a few months of one another in back-to-back years. Each of their husbands, in his own way, was sick and controlling. Anne used to have to iron the day's newspaper before her husband came home from work, because if there were wrinkles in it he would think she might have read it before him, which was reason enough for a beating. She wore her hair tied back as tightly as possible so that he couldn't grab it as he walked by her and bash her head into a table, door, or wall. If he had to dig in his pocket for his key to open their front door when he got home, he always searched the house in a rage, assuming the reason it was locked was because she had been with some other man. It was morning on a Good Friday when she rang the refuge about coming in with her two year-old daughter, because she knew that when her husband came home that night, he would kill her. She didn't have the money for a taxi and she was too afraid even to use her real name on the phone but the woman on the other end of the line at the refuge told her not to worry about anything – if she got into a taxi with her daughter, they would come out to meet her and pay the fare and she could leave if she decided she didn't like it. When she arrived and saw all the latches on the door, she finally felt safe, knowing her husband couldn't get to her there.

Anne's life with her husband was so tortured and he was so abusive that she used to pray that he would spend hours in the pub at night and then get on his bicycle (actually her bicycle) and get hit by a bus. Unlike the husbands of a lot of other women, Anne's husband's rages and tantrums weren't linked to alcohol. She could picture the Garda coming to her door holding the crumpled bicycle with the sad news of her husband's death. She knew she would have to look distraught and wondered if she could manage it.

Anne's fantasy of her husband's death reminds Sheila of a similar incident when she thought she might actually be rid of her own vicious husband. A Garda really did come to her door one night with the crumpled frame of her husband's bicycle. He had been hanging on to the back of a lorry to catch a lift and was caught off-guard when the truck made a turn. She went to the hospital, unsure of his condition. When she arrived, the first thing she saw was him walking towards her and her heart sank. She knew she couldn't show it. The worst jealousy she ever felt of another person was when a woman at the refuge got the news that her abusive husband had committed suicide. 'Now she's rid of him and she gets a widow's pension,' she remembers thinking.

One of Sheila's husband's last rages before she left to go to the refuge was over a new cooker her family had given her for her birthday. He simply didn't like the idea of their giving her such gifts. Sheila's family helped her pack the night she left her husband and unlike Anne, who took only a bag of nappies for her baby, Sheila's impulse was to take everything they could carry. She felt her husband had contributed nothing to the house, so he should be left with nothing, not even his own clothes, which she herself packed into big black bags. She even wanted to take the curtain rods because her mother had given them to her but her family insisted on putting some limits on what she would take.

The cars of Sheila's family members formed a small caravan carrying the household things, herself and her two daughters, making its way along the canal en route to the refuge. It was a lovely calm September night and the canal was smooth as glass. She doesn't remember whose idea it was but she watched the first of the black bags full of her husband's clothes gliding along the canal like great dark swans.

Her husband had come from an abusive family but he had promised her when they got married that he would never do to her what his father had done to his mother. She knows now that when she decided to marry him, she made one of the worst mistakes that women of all ages all over the world make every single day – she looked at a man, saw his serious flaws and thought, 'I can change him.' It took her years to figure out but she eventually realised that there was no changing this man.

Mary's husband may have been the most vicious of the three, although it's difficult to assign degrees to such brutality. One night after he had battered her, she sat on the bed holding a towel up to her face to stop the blood. Her children were around her, upset and crying. Her husband came into the room – she laughs at this now – and she was sure he was going to start round two. Instead he sat down next to her, put his arms around her and said, 'You know if anyone ever laid a finger on you, I'd kill them.' Mary has four children, the two eldest from a previous relationship and the two youngest with her husband. Mary found out later that he was sexually abusing the younger ones. She was so distraught by the time she moved into the refuge with her children that when I first met her, she could barely speak to me or look me in the eye. She needed to have Sheila, whom she had quickly befriended, to translate for her. Her husband showed up at the refuge more than once, trying to get at the children, terrorising them all. Once, when she actually did speak to him, he handed her pieces of her parents' gravestones that he had smashed with a hammer and wrapped up in a one-pound note 'for luck'. In other words, he hoped she was going where they were. Anne's husband succeeded in kidnapping their two year-old daughter from the refuge. One of the workers there tried to stop his car as it was leaving, injuring her arm trying to get at the door as he sped away. They got her daughter back safely within a short space of time but the women were under constant, almost unbearable levels of stress, even within the relative safety of the refuge.

The refuge manager during Sheila, Mary and Anne's time, before Kathy took over the position, was a woman named Wenda Edwards. If any of the women was particularly upset about something, she was called into Wenda's office for a chat to see if things could be straightened out. Consciously or not, Wenda had a colour-coded system of handing out tissue roll to the distraught woman, depending on the severity of the problem. 'If someone was having a really bad time of it, crying their eyes out, she got the tissue roll with the red dots,' Mary says. 'If it wasn't that bad, she got green.' If a woman came out of the office dabbing her eyes with the red-dotted paper, there was usually a sharp intake of breath from everyone outside, as they wondered what had just happened.

The women who stuck together in the refuge also showed up to support one another on their various court dates. If any of them had the misfortune of being assigned a particularly ignorant judge, the presence of her friends was even more important than usual. There was one judge nobody wanted and if a woman got him, she knew she was in trouble. No matter what the details of the case were, he never seemed to consider the possibility that it wasn't the woman's problem to work out. 'Go to Bewley's with him,' this judge told Sheila at one of the hearings after listening to whatever fresh horrors her husband was putting her through. 'And have a nice cup of coffee and a bun and you'll work it out.'

'It couldn't be just a cup of coffee,' Sheila laughs today. 'It had to be a bun, too.' Years later she did go to Bewley's for coffee and a bun, but instead of meeting her husband, she met her friend Anne and they both celebrated being made permanent in their own flats. The women had all heard the story about the same judge's recommendation to another abused wife that she put up a sign in her bedroom reading 'Peace and Charity'.

After a long time and countless court appearances, I got separations finalised for all the women. The refuge had helped to find flats for them and their children, which was a good start to beginning a life free of their abusive husbands. But once they were on their own in their new places, Sheila, Mary and Anne knew that other problems had just begun. All were short of money and although none of them were afraid of working like Trojans, first they needed to find jobs. They had little experience of work and long gaps in their employment history. Although they were grateful for them, their flats were tiny and located in areas rife with drugs and violence, which made protecting their children all the more challenging, although from different threats from before. Although all three of them knew that it was a godsend to get the chance to start over without their husbands, they were still newly single mothers whose families were trying to get out from under the dark shadow the men had cast over them.

I knew they needed extra help and in between work and other court cases I used to visit them regularly. Mary was still so wary of men that her children made a habit of clustering protectively around her if a man entered the house. But they learned quickly that I was different. They even trusted me enough to let me be the impartial judge of their mother's rules for them. Mary, like Sheila and Anne, was unsure of herself, especially in disciplining her children, when she was first settling in after leaving the refuge. She often asked for my advice and her children knew it. If they thought she was being outrageously severe, they would ask her to call me, tell me the situation and see what I said. They always stood by their promise that even if I agreed with their mother, they'd accept my decision.

I would come around to them every so often with hampers full of tinned food and small presents for the children, which left them absolutely beside themselves with anticipation of my next visit. They would ask their mothers when I was coming again and after I'd leave, they'd open and close the presses again and again so that they could see them full. They never knew exactly what I'd bring on my next visit. Sometimes, if I'd just got paid, had given Evelyn money for the week and still had some left over, I'd visit one of the women and try to give her a few pounds if she'd take it. I was no Syl Collins, though – I wouldn't have thought of grabbing one of them, stuffing it down her bra and running out the door, so I just had to give it to them outright and usually awkwardly, and hope they'd take it. Kathy Moore used to say that when I got paid, everyone got paid. For years, she and I routinely reached into our pockets at the same time, pooling our money to see if we had enough for petrol or lunch together.

There was one period of a few weeks when I brought the women great blocks of frozen beef. Through an EU scheme designed to benefit charitable causes, I was able to get high-quality surplus meat for nothing if I was able to find somewhere to store it. So I set up an arrangement with a local supermarket to use its walk-in freezers and set about carving it up with my son, Frank, to distribute it. There was so much of it that I used to take some to the old Kilfenora neighbours, too. If they weren't at home, I left it sitting on the doorstep – it was frozen solid and it would be frozen for hours. Mrs Sullivan saw me making a delivery one day and asked brashly and not a little threateningly, where hers was. I told her I was just getting to her. Some things never change and isn't that lovely?

I liked giving advice to Sheila, Mary and Anne about their children but I was waiting for the time when they'd be confident enough to disagree with me and stand their own ground. People often compare the kind of dramatic transformations that Sheila, Mary and Anne went through after such trauma to the process of a butterfly emerging from its cocoon. But most of the butterfly's metamorphosis is concealed from the world until it mysteriously emerges, a completely different creature from the way it began. The way that Sheila, Mary and Anne became independent, confident, wonderful women was different as I was able to watch them blossoming before my eyes. It was a long, slow process but each of them made it in her own time.

Mary's story has a particularly romantic twist. She was very young and unmarried when she got pregnant with her first daughter and instead of marrying her partner, she broke it off with him and he emigrated to England. After she was out of the refuge and settled for a long while, he wrote to their daughter just before her twenty-first birthday and said he'd love to meet her. He flew over from England and they met and got on very well. He explained to her that he had never got married because he had loved no one except her mother. Mary and he are still together today, which makes for a very happy ending. The couple was in a pub recently when a stranger approached them with a drink for each of them. 'It's so rare that you see couples that look really happy together that when I saw you, I had to buy you each a drink,' he said. Mary's partner joked that the drinks were probably drugged but when I heard the story I said, 'Now there's someone who has a lovely mind.'

If Mary passes through Rathmines in a taxi, she automatically gets a homey kind of feeling going by the refuge. Sheila and Anne feel the same about the place that gave them a second chance. That's part of the reason the three remain such good friends so long after they lived there together. Every now and then Kathy Moore will go into a pub and hear a loud voice in a broad accent call out to her, 'Kathy! Kathy! Howya? It's me, such-and-such from the refuge!' Many women have no problem with people knowing they spent time there but not everyone feels that way. Some of the women who've stayed there don't want to keep in touch with anyone they met there once they've left. They'd rather forget the whole experience, move on and start over from scratch.

I know some people assume that the majority of the women from the refuge whose cases I take don't have any money but that's far from true. I do many of the cases pro bono and I've depended on barristers for a lot of assistance over the years. Among them are Barbara Seligman BL, Catherine White BL, Catherine Lucy-Neale BL, Una Furlong BL, both junior and senior counsel, who've done a great deal of free work for me on behalf of women in the refuge. But years ago I took one case connected with the refuge in relation to a separation and property settlement that involved very large sums, so large, in fact, that I said to the woman, 'Your house must have a bidet.' When the case was over, she phoned and invited me for coffee, giving me a card with a bonus cheque and a photograph of not one but two bidets in her house.

The idea of suicide followed some women through the door of the refuge and never left them in peace. There was a familiar pattern that many of the abusive husbands followed, by which they tried to mend fences with their estranged wives. Firstly, it was the promise of change and a better life, the, 'Please come back, I can't live without you,' approach. When that didn't work, it was more of the same old threats against the women. Finally, it was the threat of their own suicides. If these men had any sense at all they would have realised that what they thought was a 'threat' of suicide to their wives was actually a great incentive for them to remain separated. So many men threatened to come to the refuge to top themselves that the women put up a sign that said, 'This way to the canal,' with an arrow showing the right direction. Many of these were false threats but there was one occasion when the women were outside in the early afternoon, grimly washing away blood that had poured from a pair of slit wrists before the children returned from school to see it.

There was one woman in the refuge for whom I drafted a standard letter to her husband announcing her intention to seek a separation in the courts. Her complaints against her husband hadn't struck me as particularly startling but she simply wasn't happy in the marriage and I agreed to act for her. Within two hours of receiving the letter, the woman's husband had killed himself.

I was devastated but, in the refuge, tragedy's twin was humour. The women in the refuge all heard about the incident and came flocking to me, asking me to draw up exactly the same letter for their husbands. I said to them, 'Oh, I couldn't, they're very expensive,' although in truth, I always did them free of charge. 'Doesn't matter,' the women told me. 'We'll get a loan from the credit union. It'll be worth it if he tops himself.'

There was another woman in the refuge for whom I acted

whose husband was a transvestite. One Monday afternoon, I was due in court to represent her. In the days before mobile phones, my office needed to find a way to deliver some crucial news to me about the case. They finally rang a barrister who they knew was usually in the Law Library to give me the message that the transvestite had committed suicide the previous day by throwing himself in the Liffey. 'Great, we'll win today!' I said. So we did a strike-out. Afterwards I decided I'd better go up to the refuge to pay my respects to the widow.

The transvestite always wore a denim shirt with jeans and a medallion and was a real 'bleedin' man about town, a hard man. But underneath his masculine outfits, he wore knickers and suspender belts. When I got to the refuge, the women were literally celebrating the man's demise. I went up to his wife and said, 'I believe he didn't drown.'

'What do you mean he didn't drown?' she replied, panic rising in her voice.

'I heard he caught his suspender belt on a nail going down and was hung by the goolies!' I said.

'Jaysus, for a minute I thought he wasn't dead!' she said, with relief.

I acted for another woman whose husband was a transvestite. The man was leaving his wife penniless while he was out buying the most expensive women's knickers and shoes for his own pleasure. If they'd been the same size, at least she could have got some use out of them too!

Veteran *Irish Times* journalist and women's liberation activist Mary Maher wrote an article about the refuge for its one-year anniversary in which she called me '…the only legal person universally and warmly praised,' by the women she interviewed there. Just as Mary saw me in a different category entirely from other men, the women in the refuge knew that I was no threat.

I rang at the entrance one day when everyone was jittery because of a husband's recent attempt to break in. Someone who didn't know me said from behind the door, 'It's a man!' but one of the other women replied, 'That's not a man, that's Frank Crummey.' I took that as the highest compliment.

Kathy Moore went one better than that. 'Frank, I meant to tell you,' she said to me one day as we walked to lunch in Rathmines. 'The worker here with the curly black hair said to me the other day, 'You know that small grey-haired man who comes in here all the time? I know he's a priest but what's his name?" Kathy had trouble finishing her sentence without snorting with laughter.

'Wow,' I said, 'I think I would have made a good priest.'

11

My Days in Court

If I had ever thought I was going to get a break from the more bizarre elements of society through working in the legal profession, I would certainly have been disappointed. I had met off-beat people in every one of my jobs. The law was no exception.

At first, Paul McNally gave me a wood-panelled office that was about six foot square within the Coughlan McNally firm. I quickly realised I had to be very careful about my meetings, even with the door closed, because everything could be heard out in the corridor. Paul wanted to keep me on because I was generating money for the firm with the number of conveyances I was bringing in. As long as I could be a bit profitable, Paul was happy to leave me to my own devices.

I was with Coughlan McNally for only about a year before the two solicitors decided to go their own separate ways, breaking up the firm and leaving me jobless again. I could have gone back to the buildings but I liked working in the law. I just needed a firm to attach myself to.

Shortly after Coughlan McNally broke up, while I was still at a loose end, I was chatting with a good friend, an auctioneer named Harry Perry. Since we had met years before, I think Harry was impressed by my self-confidence. 'The boy is here,' Harry would announce with a fanfare when I walked into a room. 'How is the boy?' From someone else, that might have sounded snide but I knew Harry meant it affectionately. Now, hearing that I was out of a job, he thought he could help me. He knew a solicitor, Richard McGuinness, who might be willing to take on an ageing legal executive with no firm.

Richard, a solicitor who specialises in personal injury, probate and conveyancing, had upstairs rooms in his offices that needed refurbishing. They were mine if I wanted them. Richard never once mentioned the matter of rent in the many pleasant years we worked together. Along with the rooms, Richard gave me an opportunity for a career that otherwise might have ended before it began.

I began to see myself learning how to practise law in much the same way that skilled tradesmen learn their crafts by pairing themselves with more experienced workers. I saw myself doing law as an apprenticeship, carrying out the procedures and always listening and learning. I knew that if I made a mess of a case, it would be perceived that it was because I was a legal executive and not a lawyer, whereas if a solicitor made the same mistakes, the situation would be looked upon much more forgivingly. Being an underdog in the law was the best thing for my motivation. I couldn't afford to be mediocre because I couldn't make mistakes and get away with them.

Legal executives and solicitors differ in their levels of education. Solicitors have obviously completed law school while legal executives may not have done so and they often do the bulk of their work within the office instead of in the courtroom. Many legal executives specialise in areas that lend themselves to office work, like conveyancing, probate and personal injuries. There are, of course, exceptions and I suppose I'm one. Another legal executive colleague has worked on many of the major murder trials in the country and most people don't know she's not a fully-fledged solicitor. She is as good as any solicitor.

In the past, one of the biggest problems that legal executives had was that they weren't allowed to challenge a jury on behalf of the accused. 'Challenging' a jury is the process of selecting jurors. They could attend counsel throughout a murder trial but when it came to the jury, they had to wait for the principal solicitor from their firm to come to the courtroom to go through the process. In my family law work, I don't generally deal with juries but I was nonetheless convinced that it made sense to grant legal executives the right to challenge juries themselves, not least because it was much more efficient than having to call a solicitor in for that one specific purpose. I decided I'd try to change that rule.

Along with another legal executive, Peter Doyle, who worked with Pearts, one of the city's old, beautiful firms, I had already formed a group called the Institute of Legal Executives. Doyle was the one who actually came up with the idea to form such a group and I was all for it. I put up the twenty quid or so as start-up money and it took a long time to get it going but the Institute has many members today and is held in high esteem by the Law Society.

Through the Institute, I made an appointment with a specific judge, Frank Roe (1920-2003), who was the president of the Circuit Court at the time. It was a well-known fact that Judge Roe was in favour of finishing proceedings in his court as quickly and efficiently as possible. During our meeting, I told Judge Roe I had a suggestion that might speed things along even more: why not grant legal executives the right to challenge juries? 'I never even thought of that,' Judge Roe said to me. 'And you're telling me it will make things quicker?'

'Yes,' I said.

'I'll make a statement tomorrow,' Judge Roe said. 'And I'll change it.'

It was as easy as that. The judge was true to his word and from the next day on, legal executives had the right to challenge juries just like any solicitor.

The Institute of Legal Executives has come a long way since its foundation twenty-one years ago. Legal executives now have the right to fix dates, adjourn cases and rule settlements. It has also been ruled in the High Court that legal advice given by an experienced legal executive is on a par with that of a solicitor.

The Institute of Legal Executives works very closely with Griffith College, which does wonderful work in educating young law students to a very high standard. The Institute has set up an award for the student who achieves the highest marks in their final exams. I was very pleased and honoured when they called it the 'Frank Crummey Perpetual Trophy'. I have great pleasure in presenting it each year.

The question of family law cases being heard in private is often discussed. I believe that the press should be allowed in. It would stop judges making outrageous statements such as I have heard them doing. Having said this, I have also had the pleasure of appearing before family law judges such as Judge King, Judge Crowley and Judge Furlong in the District Court and in the Circuit Court, Judge Catherine McGuinness (who was promoted to the Supreme Court and is now President of the Law Reform Commission) and Judge Michael White, all of whom showed great compassion for the women and men before them. There were many other good judges in all the courts but these were the individuals who stood out for me.

As a legal executive, I still tend to find myself in bizarre situations with unusual clients. For instance, there was the separation I worked on in which a man stripped down to complete nakedness in my office before commencing his business. The man's wife, a foreigner, was my client and she was so beautiful that if she had been the one naked in front of me, I still would have been looking only at her face. The man had naturally hired a different solicitor. It was somewhat unusual for another solicitor's client to come to my office to sign the necessary papers for a relatively simple separation but I knew the man's solicitor well and didn't think much of it.

The man arrived at my office fully dressed but within minutes of coming through my door, he had taken off his coat, pants, shirt, underwear and finally, each sock, before sitting down. I'm not a man who is easily shocked but even I was thrown by the cool demeanour of the now stark-naked man sitting before me. I blinked a few times and collected myself.

'Can I ask you why you just took off all your clothes?' I asked politely.

'This is the way I looked when I met my wife in Crete,' the man replied.

'Fair enough,' I said, looking back down and shuffling through my papers. A few moments later, I noticed that my bare visitor was gazing out the window. He turned back to me and said, 'May I use your window?'

'For what?' I asked.

'To jump out of,' he said.

'You won't be able to kill yourself from this window,' I said pragmatically and not entirely unsympathetically. 'The ledge is too big.' It wasn't the man's last suicide attempt. Shortly afterwards, he threatened to jump from the balcony of an apartment and in a fit of characteristic practicality, his neighbours began moving their parked cars from around the edges of the building. He never did end up jumping but his separation, which had caused him so much grief, was inevitably made final.

I had been through other experiences of people stripping in front of me in my own office. Years earlier, while still with the ISPCC, I was trying to help a couple who had terrible, violent arguments. The husband and wife came in to my office together one day to talk. Each attempted to outdo the other in explaining to me how persecuted they were within the relationship. The competition started innocently enough given the circumstances but it quickly escalated.

'Look at this,' the wife said, pulling up her shirt to reveal a large bruise.

'That's nothing compared to these bite marks,' said the husband, pulling off his shirt entirely. My office window was open and there was a large building site next door. As the man and woman stripped down to their underwear within the next minute and a half, shouting at each other and at me alternatively as I sat motionless at my desk, I noticed the activity on the building site grind to a halt as men in hard hats pointed fingers up to the show that was being enacted in my office.

'All right, I've seen enough!' I said hastily. 'Jesus.' The two were in their underwear and showing no signs of slowing down. The men on the building site were enjoying themselves immensely and catcalls drifted up to my window.

As I got more experienced at doing separations, I discovered that the women in the refuge weren't the only ones who didn't seem to see me as a man in the traditional sense. Through the years my clients have been overwhelmingly female and some of the things they confide in me about their personal lives and reasons for leaving a marriage remind me that no matter how much experience any one person has, no one has heard it all. One client I remember well has never been matched for her bluntness. When I asked her why she wanted a separation, she replied with complete aplomb, 'He's useless in the bed.'

I drafted the standard letter to her husband. I'd say the guy got the letter in the morning post, ran out, jumped on his bicycle and was at my office half an hour later saying, 'Where do you want me to sign?' Of course, I hadn't any agreement drafted yet. The woman had recounted to me, in great detail, all her efforts to rekindle even the faintest romantic ember. It wasn't that she didn't try, she told me – she had even got a video about love-making out of the video shop and brought it home for them to watch together. But he had dismissed it as 'disgusting' and wanted no part in anything like that. So she decided to try seduction just one more time, which elicited only the unoriginal, disappointing reply, 'I have a headache.'

'So,' she told me, 'I decided to get one of those things for myself that goes 'buzz.''

'You mean a vibrator?' I confirmed matter-of-factly.

'Yeah,' she said. The thing that had finally made up her mind about going through with the separation was the fact that her husband had told their daughter about the vibrator one day when the family was all together in their kitchen.

The separation went through and the husband couldn't wait to add his name to the document to make it official. Afterwards, I went to the Clarence Hotel with the barrister for lunch.

We walked in and the next thing, over in the corner, I see our client with her best friend and her daughter.

'There you are, Frank!' she shouted to me from across the lounge. 'Jeez, it'll be great now, here's to the vibrators!' It takes a lot to embarrass me but the tips of my ears were a little red that afternoon.

One thing I've found particularly intriguing in my legal work over the years is the way that some of my more religiously observant clients count on the Church for a good result in court. I'd love to be in a similar situation to the various saints to which my clients direct their prayers. If the clients receive a good result, they always praise the saints for answering their prayers. But if it's a bad result, the saints are immune from blame, which usually falls to the nearest mortal involved.

I once acted for a very nice woman on a case for which the barrister and I worked feverishly. We had great success and she was absolutely delighted.

'I knew St Anthony wouldn't let me down,' she said to me right after the case had ended. This couldn't help but dim my enjoyment of the victory slightly. 'Well, fuck you and St Anthony, love,' I thought. 'What about me?' What I actually said was,

'Excuse me, love, what's St Anthony got to do with your case today?' She didn't have an immediate reply to that and I thought it best to let the matter drop. I wasn't really angry anyway. I just think it's astounding that people are so sure God and the saints have a personal interest in their individual legal proceedings, the same way that celebrities or sports stars thank God when they accept an award or win a match. After years of hearing my clients' friends and family members reassuring them that Jesus will be with them in court, I've learned to resist the urge to ask if they think Jesus would like to take the stand in their friend's or relative's favour.

I like to think I'm tough enough but I was scared when my doctors told me I had to go in for heart bypass surgery shortly before my sixtieth birthday. Naturally, my friends and family were also nervous but for slightly different reasons. I knew I wasn't ready to die yet and the possibility of it frightened me but I wasn't at all ambivalent about the question of God and the afterlife. I don't believe in God, so therefore, for me, there's no question of whether or not there's an afterlife.

As I was settling into my work as a legal executive I started having chest pain severe enough to make me go to the doctor for tests. After my first stress test, I went back to work for several days while I waited for the results. I was planning to go ten-pin bowling with friends on a Friday night when I got an urgent message from my doctor that I was to do nothing but rest all weekend and then go to see the specialist on Monday.

The specialist wanted me in the hospital straight away but my daughter Edel's wedding to Mick Brophy was that Friday and there was no way I was going to miss it, even if they had to have a defibrillator at the altar. I got a prescription from the specialist and went to the local pharmacist whom I had known for years, Neville Thom, to have it filled. When I got there Neville's wife was behind the counter. She looked at the prescription and said to me, 'Do you mind waiting outside? I don't want you dying here in the shop on me.'

I made it to Edel's wedding but barely. I went into the hospital the next week. Unlike the time I had my nervous breakdown, I had VHI medical insurance but it wasn't enough. When the doctor asked me if I could put up another thousand pounds to make up the difference for the cost of my surgery and his care, I knew the right answer was, 'Yes.' Even though Evelyn and I still didn't have much money, I knew this particular thousand pounds was worth getting.

The surgery did not go well. I went in for the bypass, came out and was back on the operating table again with my chest opened up for the second time in twenty-four hours. They sent for the family and gave them tea and biscuits. You know when they give your family tea and biscuits, you're going to die. There had been a serious problem with the first surgery and the odds weren't in favour of my surviving the second.

When I woke up the second time, the pain in one of my arms was unbearable. The doctor told me the surgical team had had to jerk the arm out of the way very quickly to get a better angle at something. I didn't care to spend much time imagining what had gone wrong. For one thing, I was in too much pain and for another, I was contented to be alive.

I had lots of visitors in my room in Our Lady's Nursing Home in Dalkey. One of them was Kathy Moore, who walked in one day with a large brown paper bag. When I opened it, I found £2,016 and some change in cash. The women in the refuge had held a fundraising night for me to help with my medical bills and to keep me and Evelyn going while I recuperated.

The painting that hung over my nursing home bed was of the Sacred Heart of Jesus. Gory in even its tamest depictions, the colouring in this particular Sacred Heart distressed me. The face was blue. If anyone ever looked like he needed a bypass, it was Jesus in this painting. When Syl Collins and his wife Frances came in to visit me for the first time, they turned the painting to the wall so I wouldn't have to look at it. A nun came in shortly afterwards to let me know when the Masses were scheduled, saw the new position of the painting and must have decided on the spot that I was a lost cause as far as Mass was concerned.

As most of my close friends are lifelong Catholics of varying degrees of devoutness, I was questioned, usually gently, about my thoughts on religion and death. Two people in particular came in to see me and said, 'Can I ask you a personal question?' When I heard that, I knew it was going to be something about God.

'Did you ask for the priest?' they'd say in hushed tones.

'Well, of course not. I'm not in the club. Why would I?' I'd reply.

But my questioners were genuine people and they'd say to me, 'Well, I'll keep praying. I'll keep praying for you.'

I think a lot of the people who like me don't want me, in the end, to be left out. My friend Padraic Mac Ionnraic from my Australia adventure had an interesting insight for me when he himself was dying.

'I'm looking forward to heaven,' Padraic said to me one night when he was visiting. 'The only one thing that depresses me is that you won't be there.'

I thought about that one for a minute. 'You know, Padraic, if I'm not there, it won't be heaven!' I finally said.

We talked about other things that night too. Mostly, we shared the feeling that I think of as being in the departure lounge and hoping our flights will be delayed. Or that it will happen to be a Ryanair flight and we won't have the proper identification.

I'm still puzzled that some people assume atheists have nothing to live for. I think being an atheist has actually simplified my life by removing all religious factors from my moral philosophy. All I want to do is to leave this world a little better for my being here. I believe that what you can do for good or evil in this world is minute; otherwise you're infinitely overestimating your own importance. But I think it is important that you try to do something for the good.

Recently, around my seventieth birthday, I found myself in and out of doctor's offices again, being poked and prodded and having to undergo more heart tests. I had an angiogram, a procedure where dye is injected into an artery so that doctors can see if there are any cardiac irregularities. It's not uncommon for patients to experience cardiac arrest during such tests, which I did. The last thing I remember before my heart stopped was that my face felt very warm and then, nothing. The next thing I knew, a woman was poised to bring the paddles back down on my chest and I heard a voice say, 'He's back!'

My son Frank asked me if there had been any sign of long tunnels, bright lights, spinning flowers and ethereal music – all the standard near-death experiences. I don't remember anything like that – just the warmth in the face, a report that prompted more than one person to wonder – out loud and in my presence – if they should be asking me about flames and brimstone rather than music and soft lights.

Sometimes it seems to me that there's a lot of competition between people of different religions for the souls of atheists. It's like we're the swing voters who might help a politician win an election. A group of Jehovah's Witnesses frequent my house, probably because I welcome them in, let them talk and sometimes make them breakfast. They think they have a chance. Actually, they have two chances: fuck all and none! But I admire anybody – I don't care what they advocate – who gets up day after day, month after month, knocking on people's doors, getting told to fuck off. You've got to give them some credit for it. That's something I can relate to from my days in Reform, the LFM and the family planning movement.

Friends of mine from long ago, those who are still devout

Catholics, worry about my soul and how I'll fare in God's eyes on judgement day. Such matters inevitably arise with much more frequency when I'm in the hospital. Sometimes people appeal to Evelyn to intervene with me but she knows better. Although she is still a believer, she's not the slightest bit worried that I'm not. Recently, an old friend of ours tried to convince Evelyn to go to the nuns with an offering in my name so I could re-enter the Church before I die.

'If you feel like doing it, you go over,' Evelyn said.

'I would, if you give me the money,' the woman replied.

There was one instance I remember fondly, many years ago, when a friend of mine thought the perfect chance for the prodigal son to return to the fold was lost. I was driving home from work and the traffic was horrendous, so instead of sitting in it and going nowhere, I decided to get off the road and wait it out for a while. I drove into Mount Argus, parked the car and entered the church, sitting down quietly at a pew in the back.

There was no Mass on but one woman from the area who knew me and my unorthodox contrary views spotted me, came over and loudly proclaimed, 'The cheek of yeh in God's house! Get out!' Rather than argue with her, or, as I remember it, being a coward and being prudent, I simply got up and left. A few days later, I told the story to Patty, the wife of my friend Declan Walsh, who was very religious and involved in Church activities. She was horrified. I had been accosted on the first occasion on which I'd entered a church on my own and not for a wedding or a funeral in years – not very Christian on that woman's part, she observed. She told one of the priests about it and he made a point of dropping in to tell me that I was welcome in the church whenever I wanted to come.

The hypocrisy I experienced in some of the most devout Catholics in Ireland that was much worse than one woman's pettiness in putting me out of Mount Argus.

During my children's school years, I had plenty of run-ins with their teachers but there was one nun in particular whose behaviour managed to irritate me so much that I ended up getting my solicitors to send her a letter.

Evelyn and I had several clashes with this nun. One was due to the fact that she had cut one of our children's hair in school, without consulting us at all, because she thought it was too long. I wasn't in Dublin at the time but Evelyn went up to the school to intervene. Shortly after that incident, our eldest daughter Elizabeth was very ill in hospital, in a coma. It had all started with severe flu symptoms and she had become dehydrated. When she got to the hospital, she was given several injections and lost consciousness. I had a look at the chart hanging at the foot of her bed to discover that they had given her Largactil, a drug I was familiar with from my experience in social work. I knew the dosage wasn't suitable for her weight or age. I went out to find the consultant in charge of her care and confronted him.

'You know about drugs?' the consultant asked me uncomfortably.

'Enough,' I said.

Elizabeth was put in a private room with a private nurse as the hospital attempted to compensate for its mistake. She was in a coma for days and the doctors didn't have much concrete information for us. For a while, they said, everyone would just have to wait and see.

Back at the children's school, the head nun heard about Elizabeth's condition and sent a little girl around to all the classrooms to tell the teachers to have their classes pray for her recovery. When the little messenger got to this particular nun's classroom with the request, the nun launched into an angry, self-righteous speech against the Crummeys.

'Sister Claire said to pray for Elizabeth Crummey,' the messenger girl said.

'I might,' replied the nun. She went on to explain to the class that Elizabeth's mother had been all right until she had married me but now neither of us were of any use. I also recall that she expressed her opinion that God knew who to send these kinds of misfortunes to and that the Crummeys had it coming to them.

I received an account of the nun's speech from my niece, Paula Ormsby, who was sitting in the front row of the class when it was delivered. She's a very clever girl so she knew, 'You don't say that about my uncle.' She came home and loyally reported what she had heard back to me. In the midst of my worry about Elizabeth, I was angry enough to place a phone call to my solicitors to request that they send a letter to this nun. The gist of the letter was that if Evelyn and I hadn't received an apology within three days, we would proceed for defamation without further notice.

You can picture the nuns getting a solicitor's letter. There was bedlam.

We were inundated with good wishes from various members of the religious community. One of the other nuns wrote a letter to us saying what wonderful parents we were and that God had chosen us to bear this cross because of it. Then we had a priest call down to us, a man I knew very well, Father John Francis. He was so upset and we were lovely people and the nuns were so upset and so on. Finally, the letter of apology arrived from the nun herself. I didn't give a fuck. I was just putting her back in her box. I heard stories later from parents of other children in that nun's classes that only reinforced my low opinion of her. One mother told the nun that her young daughter was waking up in the middle of the night with nightmares about her. To reassure the mother, the nun said she would be especially nice to her daughter. Instead, she went into class and proclaimed how silly it was for a little girl to wake up saying, 'I hate my teacher.' A different child from the one whose mother had just spoken to the nun piped up tearfully and said, 'I didn't mean it, Sister!'

They were all having nightmares, waking up saying they hated her.

How does someone gauge the evolution of something as intangible as religious belief throughout their lives? When they encounter a believer who morphs into a non-believer and vice versa, people always want to know about the moment of recognition when the mind actually pivoted and changed. A life itself can change radically or end altogether in an instant, as I knew from my London bus accident and my father's death. But the story of how an altar boy from Kilfenora who used to sing hymns at the top of his lungs became an atheist is too complex to explain as hinging on a single moment or event. It was as if my years in the LFM, Reform and the contraception movement had been priming me for my time in the Kylemore, the first time in my life when I really stepped back to sort out my feelings about some of the big questions. Other people probably sensed how I felt even before I knew myself. There was a reason the nuns vanished from the schoolyard when I appeared there.

When I had the nervous breakdown I realised I had to make some serious adjustments and ask myself certain questions: one of them was about religion. I focused on the conclusion that I'd been coming to over years and decided that religion was an absolute load of twaddle. I came to that realisation with no trepidation. While I was in the nursing home, I knew one of my Belfast aunts on my father's side would send one of the Franciscan monks to visit me and I had no intention of entertaining him. I said to the matron, 'If you see anybody coming in to visit me that looks like a priest but particularly with a rope around his belly, I'm not available.' I wasn't worried about what would be a suitable excuse for being 'unavailable' as a patient in the psychiatric ward but at that point, meeting the Franciscan was the last thing I needed.

Two of my father's sisters, Cissie and Mary, had been raised in one of the most ultra-traditional Irish Catholic moulds imaginable, even for the era. My grandmother hadn't allowed either of them to marry. Simple as that: they had to stay at home and look after her. As I remember, that kind of arrangement was common in those days. I would call to the house in Fairview where the three women lived and my aunt Mary, the younger of the two, would answer the door wearing an apron with flour on it because she'd been baking little scones and cakes in anticipation of my visit. She was a lovely, lovely person and I loved her to bits. Cissie was the tougher of the two and, when I was at the height of my public profile criticising the Church and the Christian Brothers, (and two first cousins of mine were Brothers) Cissie was not at all pleased to see me calling. If I visited with Evelyn, she couldn't even bring herself to speak to me. She would look directly at Evelyn and talk, talk, talk to her. She found it hard to even look at me. One of my first cousins, Pat Crummey, told me that he knew there were times when she could have knifed me.

Every so often, Cissie and Mary would entertain the Franciscans from Merchant's Quay in their house in Fairview. They laid out a generous spread for the priests they so revered. They prepared and served a tremendous meal in the kitchen and then brought the Franciscans into the parlour for after-dinner brandies. The image that sticks in my mind the most vividly is that of Cissie and Mary reversing out of the room after serving the priests. As an old-fashioned sign of respect, they would not turn their backs on their guests.

Although I have very few memories of my father while I was growing up, I was much closer to my father's extended family – at least the Dublin Fairview branch – than I was to my mother's. I used to play cards with my granny, my father's mother, every Thursday afternoon when I was a young boy. Unfortunately, when I grew up and word about my various rebellious activities and my stinging criticisms of the Christian Brothers drifted around to the various branches in Belfast, Luton, New Zealand and anywhere else where groups of Crummeys had settled, resentment grew in some, suspicion in others and plain old intrigue in others. Charlie and Andrew, my much younger cousins who had been born in England and lived in Scotland, told me recently that when they came to Dublin to visit years ago, they were taken around to every branch of the family except mine. I held a certain mysterious fascination for them as children: what kind of man was this that the family avoided so carefully, so deliberately? It was only when my Aunt Cissie passed away about fifteen years ago that Charlie and Andrew came over again and ended up staying with me that we began talking to each other. They told me the stories that they'd heard about me: that I was a bad influence and this and that. They've now decided that I am the most interesting of all their cousins and they want to stay in contact.

The thing for which I have to give my father's extended family credit is that although it was obvious I was not the favourite son, they weren't outwardly hostile. They would never have been impolite at a funeral or wedding…well, I wasn't invited to weddings. The first of my cousins who invited me to a wedding was Pat Crummey, although he had two brothers who were Christian Brothers. That was a break, if you know what I mean. Then my cousin Walter invited me to his wedding.

Even on the occasions when Evelyn and I visited Aunt Cissie and she acted as if I wasn't in the room, she would serve us tea and fill us in on the gossip from the various branches of the family. So I honestly harboured no ill-will towards her, even after she passed away and it came to light that she had left healthy enough sums of money to the eldest son of each family with the exception of myself. That's where she was coming from and that was all right.

I often saw Cissie throughout her final illness, buying her a wheelchair and taking her out for a day trip here and there. I was also with her when she passed away. I gave her a spoonful of brandy, which she loved, and she said, 'That's nice,' her last words, before closing her eyes and dying. I sometimes think I was too far ahead of the times for some people to catch up and

Aunt Cissie and I were never going to see eye to eye. I'd like to think that when I wasn't there, she might have managed at some stage to say something nice about me. She died before the scandals broke about priests having affairs, secretly fathering children and sexually abusing Irish children. In fairness to her, if she had lived through all that, I think it's very possible that she might have been able to admit that I'd been a little bit right in some of my criticisms and activism.

The turnout at Cissie's funeral was huge but no one had planned a eulogy or speech in her honour. When that became obvious, I figured it was up to me to stand up and say something. There was a collective gasp from the mourners when I stood to face everyone.

'The most important thing about Cissie,' I began, 'was that she was a good news person.' I paused. 'Thank God for that, from my point of view.'

The tense audience relaxed into waves of laughter. Nearly everyone at the funeral knew about my complex relationship with Cissie, so they knew exactly what I meant. My Aunt Mary had died suddenly years previously, at the young age of fifty-eight. So Cissie had become the hub of the family, the central figure who knew everyone's news. Cissie's version of the news was always delivered with the best possible shine and spin. According to her, no Crummey ever started working at the bottom of the rung. They were always managers and foremen. She used to boast to me about one cousin in particular who owned his own shop overseas with a friend and who was fabulously successful. I found out later that the shop my cousin ran was a sex boutique and he was fabulously successful, although Cissie either selectively overlooked that detail or never knew it in the first place.

Cissie and Mary had been particularly pleased when I sought out my father in London as a young bus driver and had a chance, however briefly, to speak to him again before he died. The brother whose vices they had lamented throughout their lives was still their brother, still family. To the Belfast Crummeys, family meant a great deal.

I saw other old enemies soften towards me as the years passed. Evelyn's mother, like Cissie, often preferred to act as if I was invisible but years into our marriage, she relented slightly. Every so often I would give her a lift to Mass but she still wouldn't look at me or speak to me. But when she'd get out of the car, I'd find a chocolate bar on her seat, because she knew I liked sweets.

Other family members dealt graciously with a scandal I brought upon their house as a young man. The first time I ever got arrested, I was staying with my mother's sister, my Aunt Kitty, in the Markets area of Belfast. My friend Declan Walsh and I were in Belfast for a road race. Declan and I would travel the country when we were very young doing different races. Declan was a much more talented athlete than me but it was always fun trying to keep up with him.

The Markets area of Belfast was rough. I was very fond of Kitty and she always made me spectacularly welcome, offering me a bed in her house, even if it meant that her children had to sleep on the floor.

When Declan and I got to Casement Park, the site of the race, we found it had been cancelled, so we decided to walk around for a little while. Walking down the Glen Road, I told Declan to stop and I'd take his photograph. There happened to be an RUC station in the background, which I very soon discovered was a poor choice of scenery. As soon as the flash went off, the shutters in the police station slammed shut and the doors locked up. The year was 1957, the IRA was very active and unbeknownst to us, there had been a murder in Coalisland that became known as the Coalisland booby-trap murder. The Belfast police were a little edgier than usual. RUC men came out and surrounded us and asked for our names and addresses. The man in charge was polite enough but when I reached into my pocket for identification, he drew his gun. That's when I began to get the idea that we might be in serious trouble.

We were brought into Glen Road police station where my camera was confiscated and Declan and I were questioned. We told one of the RUC men there we were up in Belfast for the race in Casement Park that had been cancelled and he had an interest in athletics, so the conversation was friendly enough. But then two cars pulled up outside and we were abruptly transferred to Springfield Road RUC station under heavy guard.

To say we were shitting bricks would be an understatement. The police had got my film developed and weren't happy with what they saw. When Declan and I had been out training, running along Divis Mountain, I had taken Declan's photograph, thinking nothing of the large television mast in the background. Enthusiastic tourist that I was, I had also taken a photo of Carrickfergus Castle as we travelled through that town. Combine these with the photo of the Glen Road RUC station and the RUC thought they were looking at a photo montage of my bombing targets.

At Springfield Road station, the interrogators were very unfriendly. We were 'little IRA bastards', and they weren't very interested in hearing that we didn't even support the IRA, never mind being members. I told them that my cousin, Malcolm McNeil, was a sergeant in the RUC. One of the RUC men pointed a gun at our heads. It had been hours since we ate anything and both of us were famished. When one RUC man told another he was going out and he'd be back in about twenty minutes, I piped up, 'Would you ever bring us back some chips?'

Declan was not amused. 'Just shut up, you,' he said to me miserably. He needn't have added, 'You're the one who got us into this mess.'

At about half-past two that morning, we were thrown out on to the street as abruptly as we'd been arrested and we weren't offered a lift. Neither of us had taxi money, so we set off for a long walk back to the Markets. I knew my Aunt Kitty would be wondering where I was. When we finally arrived back, there was great excitement, because the RUC had been there searching her house. I was worried that she would be upset about the whole thing but her reaction was the opposite. It had earned us street cred. We got the biggest, best breakfast possible the next morning.

When we got back to Dublin by train the next day, our friend was waiting for us at the station. 'What the fucking hell were you two up to, getting arrested?' he asked.

'How did you know?' we asked. It turned out that our friend's father had been on duty with the Special Branch and although there wasn't officially supposed to be any communication between the RUC in Belfast and the Special Branch in Dublin, in reality there was communication. When he received a phone call about the two young Dublin boys being held in custody, he said, 'Ah Jesus! They're all right! They're just athletes!' I never found out if that phone call was made before or after I asked for the chips.

One rule I stuck to throughout my years in the LFM, family planning, Reform and all the other organisations was that I would never put myself in a position where I was depending on income related to my activism. Many of the people I worked with at the very beginning of the family planning movement went on to careers in the field but I didn't. Part of the magic that the movements held for me was that they were something for me to do outside work and I knew they were making a difference in people's lives.

In the years after the family planning movement really got going, I opted out of it and concentrated on work and raising my family. All they needed were little mouths like me to get things started and then the tenacious workers like Doctor Jim

Loughran, Robin Cochran, Professor David McConnell, Alan McConnell, Pat O'Donovan and Doctor Derek Freedman kept it going after that.

By the time I was a legal executive, my old friend, Jim Loughran, was nearly seventy years old and considering winding down. Doctor Loughran had been running the family planning clinic at Number 10 Merrion Square for years. I suggested setting up a new clinic in 1996 and acting as its director while Doctor Loughran would be the chief physician. We contacted Marie Stopes International for advice and contacts but were unable to accept any donations from the organisation under the Abortion Information Act, as it funded clinics in Britain and elsewhere where abortions were carried out. Nonetheless, we decided to call the clinic Marie Stopes Reproductive Choices and we set it up at the same address in Merrion Square as the earlier clinic. Jim Loughran would be working within the company rather than running it himself, in his preparation for retirement.

Things went well at the clinic. Naming it Marie Stopes had been a gutsy move as it was a name that some associated with abortion but I respected the company and found it had plenty of good advice and contacts. It was acceptable and legal for the clinic to give pre-medical examinations to women who would then refer themselves to England for an abortion if they chose. There were a few company directors besides me and Jim Loughran doubled as one of them as well as being a doctor.

About a year after the clinic's opening, I was in Galway working on a family law case, eating my favourite Chicken Maryland with the barrister I was working with, when I got a call on my mobile to tell me that the clinic had been raided with a search warrant and that Doctor Loughran had been taken in by the Gardaí for questioning. I hurried back to Dublin that night and went to the clinic first thing in the morning. There were already reports in the press that 'a Dublin clinic' had been raided but it hadn't yet been named. I talked to Doctor Loughran and another director and found out that about eight Gardaí had come to take away some medical instruments, books and other materials the day before because a woman had alleged that she had had an abortion on the premises several years previously.

I asked Doctor Loughran if he had carried out an abortion and he told me he hadn't. The media had to be dealt with and as managing director of the clinic, I took on the task. I was fortunate that I had nothing to hide, because keeping track of lies in such a maelstrom of attention would have been tremendously difficult. I tried not to decline any interviews unless I had the best possible reason. I repeated the same statement endlessly – yes, it was our clinic and the doctor had told me it hadn't happened.

A few days after my media appearances, a judge stopped me outside the courts. 'I may not agree with you,' he said, 'but it's obvious you're telling the truth.' I'd been a little worried about how some of the more conservative judges might react to me in court because of the spotlight that I'd been placed under but I needn't have. I never noticed a change in their professional attitudes towards me. But this didn't mean I was in the clear.

As soon as I went on the airwaves and gave interviews to the papers and the clinic was named, protesters swarmed around Number 10 Merrion Square. I stepped out of the clinic one day to find myself inches away from a woman who was leading a large group of protesters and screaming, 'Crummey is a killer!' I recognised her. I had given her advice years before, at her request, about how to go about a termination. When I look back on pictures of myself from that time in the newspapers, I feel as if it's the oldest I've ever looked in my life. My double bypass surgery was then in the recent past and my caseload was sure to increase because of the recent introduction of divorce legalisation in the Republic. Instead of settling into an old armchair as I entered my sixties, I was building a new career and starting a new clinic. But I wasn't thirty years old any longer, even if I often felt as if I was, and stresses inevitably hit me harder than they had in the past.

After about a year, the Director of Public Prosecutions found that Doctor Loughran had no case to answer and he was cleared entirely. By that time, he had fully retired. The clinic moved from Merrion Square to a building in Blessington Street, which was a much larger space and entirely fitted out for the purpose. But the protesters followed the clinic and because nothing had come of the allegations against Doctor Loughran they were even more incensed. One group was particularly hostile, especially towards me. Members of the group plastered posters around the north side of the city with my picture, captioned, 'Crummey is a killer'. Friends very kindly went around tearing them down.

The posters didn't worry me but other things did. I was on my way to court one day with a young student from a local school doing a placement in family law when I got a call saying there was a disturbance at the clinic. Hundreds of protesters had gathered and had managed to take over parts of the clinic and Gardaí were everywhere trying to keep the peace. There was one man seated outside amidst the chaos whom I vaguely recognised. He had a doll in his arms and was singing hymns, one after another. I eventually managed to get inside the clinic with the student, where I discovered a woman who had come in that day for an appointment and was very distressed at the disturbance. The main problem was how to get her out of the clinic without the crowd harassing her.

The Gardaí offered to take her outside with her head covered and her face concealed and drive her into the city centre, away from the crowds. But we also wanted to make sure the crowd wouldn't rush the vehicle when they saw her getting into it. 'Look, they hate you,' the superintendent said matter-of-factly to me. 'You and I will go out there and distract them.'

The plan worked a little too well. We went out the back door, the crowd saw us and in a blur of motion and screaming, the Garda van parked in the lane was rolled backwards, leaving me on one side of it and the superintendent on the other. A group of protesters spotted me and I had the sickening feeling of being cornered in the face of impending attack. People rushed over and started hitting me with placards. I could do nothing but stand against the wall. There were lots of other times in my life when being small was an advantage but this time it wasn't going to save me.

One of the protesters deliberately kicked me in the chest, then righted himself with his legs spread apart. Where I came from, you got one chance like that. I kicked him in the balls. The Gardaí finally made their way around to me, forming a protective circle. When we got to safety, I found that my glasses had been broken and my finger was cut but my heart was still pumping. Vigorously, as a matter of fact. I found out later that the man I'd kicked had made a formal complaint at Fitzgibbon Street garda station that I had assaulted him. I heard the sergeant's response had been something along the lines of, 'You kicked him and he kicked you back, so you're even.'

Shortly after that day of heavy protest at the clinic, I was invited to a reception in Stormont Castle in Belfast by the Women's Coalition. I went with a friend of mine from Marie Stopes International in London, Helen Axby. We were on the third floor, having a drink and looking out the window, when we noticed a group of people who looked like protesters – not an unusual sight on the grounds of Stormont. We figured it was either a Loyalist or a Republican protest but as we were leaving, Helen pulled me aside. 'I'm impressed,' she said. 'That protest is against you.'

It was true. A Belfast group had heard I would be at Stormont and had come out against me. One of the leaders of the group was a very polite woman who approached me directly. 'I pray to God every night that you'll be forgiven before you die,' she said.

I sensed she was genuine. 'That's very nice of you,' I said.

There were 'representatives' from other hostile groups there too and a small young woman came over to me shouting obscenities. I just told her to fuck off. They followed me all the way down to Carson's statue, where I got a taxi and legged it out of there. I couldn't help feeling just a bit pleased with myself that I had angered a group of protesters enough for them to travel a hundred miles to annoy me.

I'm immensely proud of the clinic as it is today, with its new equipment and relatively luxurious conditions but it's obvious to me that using the Marie Stopes name has hurt it in some ways. For instance, the government didn't grant it medical card status. My mission statement in relation to terminations is very simple. If a woman comes to us with a crisis pregnancy, she should be treated with compassion, kindness and the best of medical attention. And whatever decision she makes is hers and hers alone. If she decides to have a termination, when she comes back, she'll be treated with compassion, kindness and the best of medical attention.

For years, I've been a regular on the debating circuit in universities all over the country on the topic of a woman's right to choose. I never expected to win a vote at the end of the debate in favour of legalising abortion but winning was never the point anyway. So I was shocked in March 2006 when I was the speaker at University College Galway in favour of legalising abortion and, for the first time, I carried the audience's vote by three. I know it's unlikely I'll see it in my lifetime but like the legalisation of contraceptives and divorce in Ireland, the legalisation of abortion is inevitable. When legal abortion does come to Ireland, I believe Marie Stopes International will have a clinic here the next day.

I know I've shocked men and women alike through the years by my sudden and utterly direct questions about their sex lives in the most everyday situations. I look at it differently; I think a lot of people are relieved to be able to talk about sex frankly and without worrying that someone will judge them. One way to elicit honest answers from people is to catch people completely off-guard. Driving through town: 'So were you a virgin before you met this partner?' Over lunch in a fancy hotel: 'Do you still enjoy making love with your husband?' Some people think I go too far with the openness. If you think about how unmentionable the topic used to be, in the not-so-distant past, I almost feel as if we have to make up for lost time for all those years when people thought talking about sex was not just taboo but sinful.

Life is not a dress rehearsal. You only have one chance here, so why not make the best of it? One of the disgraceful things about the society I grew up in was that it forbade any discussion of sex. Sex is a huge part of everybody's life. Even celibates. So there should be no embarrassment about sex. Sex should be seen as a lovely thing. People should respect one another but that doesn't mean that you shouldn't ask or answer questions. Ignorance is never bliss, in my opinion. And the number of Irish people of recent generations who grew up knowing absolutely nothing about sex still upsets me.

In my opinion, the same goes for masturbation. My re-collection of the Christian Brother demonstrating how to sleep in a non-sinful position is the perfect example of the prevailing attitude of my youth. While I'm probably not the only seventy-something year-old man who counts myself among the fans of the still-popular television series, *Sex and the City*, it's safe to say I'm not the target demographic of the show. Still, I enjoy what many critics have hailed as a ground-breaking programme for its sheer explicitness on sexual topics.

I was watching an episode the other day in which one of the women's vibrators broke down and she brought it back to the shop to change it. I was shaking with laughter, because it's wonderful that people nowadays are quite willing to talk about things like that. A dirty joke I heard a long time ago about girls' boarding schools – 'Lights out at ten, candles out at eleven!' – still makes me laugh. Long before the Ann Summers shops came to Ireland, female friends of mine used to ask me to bring them vibrators back from England. These requests were almost always made with much uneasiness and the women didn't want to use the word 'vibrator': 'Would you bring one of those things back with you?' they'd ask.

I knew the drill, so to speak, so I didn't have to work too hard to figure out what they were talking about. 'Certainly,' I'd say, coolly professional. 'And what size would you like?'

'Whatever you think yourself,' they'd whisper, anxious to finish the embarrassing exchange. I was delighted to help anyone I could with such requests and only sorry there wasn't yet any place in Ireland where the women could go themselves without having to commission a middleman.

One night I was working the switchboard at a Dublin hospital; there was absolutely nothing going on and I was quite bored. A girl walked in and asked me calmly where the casualty section was. 'Down this corridor and that set of steps,' I pointed. 'I'll send the nurse down after you.' A few minutes later, my switchboard went. It was the nurse asking me to ring for the doctor on duty, a young intern. The intern hurried down and a few minutes later, the switch went again – this time, the intern was ringing for the gynaecologist.

'What's wrong?' I said to the intern. He told me that the girl had been masturbating with a small battery and it had got caught up behind her pubic bone.

'Are her eyes flashing?' I quipped.

'That's not very nice!' the intern said, embarrassed. He told me that if this had happened down the country, they'd send for the bishop.

I wanted to make sure the intern knew that if he called the consultant out for such a simple thing, he would be very cross. 'The nurse can flick that out in a minute,' I said, which she did with no need for a consultant. The only person not embarrassed was the patient.

My frankness surprised many people but other acquaintances of mine either overcame their shyness about asking sexual questions or never experienced that shyness in the first place. There were dozens of women friends who came to me for advice before contraceptives were readily available. I always tried to sort them out and often pointed them in the direction of one of the clinics so they would know where to go for medical advice in the future. Some of the Kilfenora neighbours felt that if they had to have such an oddball in their midst, they might as well take advantage of my expertise. One young Kilfenora woman was getting married and she went to her mother for family planning advice. 'I know nothing about that,' her mother said. 'You'd better go to see Frankie Crummy.' Like all close-knit areas, the Kilfenora neighbours knew which people on the street to consult for certain things, like small repairs and carpentry. I was the resident sex-education expert.

One woman, a friend who was also a worker at the women's refuge, came to me with a family planning problem but it was the opposite of the one I was used to helping women with. This woman had been with her partner for several years and wanted children but had been unable to conceive. This woman had no obvious problem like the father-in-law sleeping in the next room but I still had advice for her, a lot of little things that she and her husband could be doing that would improve their chances, that I had picked up and remembered through my family planning campaigning. I gave her a laundry list of things ranging from the ideal temperature for her husband's showers to positions to post-coital activities to help things along. I told her that if she followed as much of my advice as possible, I'd be shocked if she weren't pregnant within a few months.

Several months later the phone rang in our house and Evelyn answered. It was the woman asking for me but I wasn't in, so Evelyn asked if there was a message.

'Please tell him thank you for getting me pregnant!' she said and hung up. Evelyn, as always, was unfazed and delivered the good news.

My friend from the refuge was delighted and she decided to go an unconventional route as it got closer to her delivery date. She wanted a natural, drug-free birth at her home with the assistance of a midwife and preferred a mobile birth, the idea of which was for the mother to be in motion, walking around, as the baby was being delivered. She also wanted the whole event documented, so she hired a photographer to come in and take still photos of the birth as it happened.

When she went into labour, all were assembled – the mother and father-to-be, the midwife and the photographer. The couple's very large dog was also present. I was summoned, too – after all, the mother figured, I had almost as much to do with this child's arrival into the world as she and her husband did – but I was working and assured her I'd make it to her house as soon as I could. As it turned out, I missed the birth itself but the story of the baby's arrival into the world is one I really enjoy.

The mother was reportedly doing very well, walking around slowly on the pillows and soft layers of blankets that lined the birthing room to cushion the baby's arrival if by some accident the midwife's grip slipped. Like a lot of mothers delivering their first child, she had been in labour for quite some time and was getting tired. The photographer was at the ready. The midwife was helping her walk. The partner was pacing. The mother-to-be had the urge to use the bathroom. Unfortunately, the baby had the urge to be born simultaneously and chose the exact moment that its mother set foot in the uncushioned bathroom to push itself out.

After hours and hours of walking around and waiting, there was a mad flurry of excitement. The midwife ran in to catch the little arrival before it hit the floor and made it, heroically, just in time. The photographer followed, frantically trying to arrange herself at a good angle to get a shot of the baby. In the process of trying to balance herself on the toilet, her foot slipped into the bowl and she twisted her ankle as she took the pictures. If it had been a play, the final scene before the curtain fell would have been of the couple's large dog trotting calmly up to the exhausted mother and beginning to lick her bottom.

After hearing the story of how the baby whose conception I aided entered the world, I'm still not sure whether or not I'm sorry to have missed it.

I was surrounded by all these mad fucking people but it was I who was the crazy one.

12

Retirement

I remember a Holy Thursday tradition as a child that we went around visiting the hospices and saying prayers for the patients. We also visited the morgue and, since children's prayers were supposed to be the purest, we'd say prayers for the dead too. On one of these Holy Thursday visits, a girl in my group brought a bag of chips into the morgue with her. When she inevitably spilled them on to one of the sheeted corpses, she gathered them back up and ate them anyway. Like I said, on Kilfenora, you didn't waste.

Death was an important part of social life on Kilfenora and during my childhood, parents made no attempt to protect children from the unpleasantness associated with it. On the contrary, children were usually deliberately included in all the activities surrounding a local death. If it was known that someone in a certain house was very ill, everyone would watch for a window to be opened. When it was, it meant that the person had just passed away and the path was being made clear for the soul to move out of the house and, presumably, up to heaven. The next day, all the neighbours, young kids included, would queue up outside the house to go inside and visit the mourning family. Among other things, it was a chance to see the inside of the neighbours' houses, which most children loved.

Back then, old people who were very sick got their funeral

shrouds from the church in advance of their deaths. If you got your shroud and wore it in your final days, it meant you were resigned to the will of God. If you had a bad turn, you put your arm in a sleeve of the shroud, said a prayer, lit a candle and received the grace of a happy death. One Kilfenora woman had so many turns that the neighbours reckoned she must have worn out the shroud before she died.

In one house, Mr Eastman had a special black shroud because he was a member of the Third Order in Mount Argus. Times were particularly lean for Mrs Eastman and the kids needed clothes. Mr Eastman, God bless him, was an old man. If he still had one sleeve of the shroud, which is all he really used of it anyway, he'd probably never be the wiser.

Harry Eastman, my friend with whom I later went to Australia, got a fine new suit for school made from the shroud. Mr Eastman went on using the sleeve and lighting candles. Everybody was happy until Mr Eastman actually did die and had only the sleeve of his black shroud in which to be buried. A story was concocted about an accident involving fire and Mount Argus was happy to oblige the family with a new shroud.

Far from being embarrassed about wearing a funeral-shroud suit, Harry Eastman is proud of his family's resourcefulness. Knowing the Mount Argus priests, I think some of them might have even been pleased that the shroud had been put to such an innovative and practical use. Harry could be fairly certain that none of the other boys would turn up to school in a suit quite like his own.

Now we're the adults and the Kilfenora neighbours Evelyn and I grew up with are getting old. The funerals for friends come more closely together with each passing year. The death of Jackie Fagan, the Kilfenora neighbour and Special Branch officer assigned to me for so many years, was one that was hard to get my head around. He followed me for so many years, I suppose it's only right that I should follow him now for something. Funerals are still occasions for reminiscences, as long as they're honest and not too sentimental, although sometimes I can't help myself being a little mushy. But the great thing about Kilfenora is that we have never lost our love for one another.

That love dictates that the worst offence you could commit against the recently deceased is their false martyrdom. It's a cardinal Kilfenora sin to make up nice things to say about the dead. It would be like erasing who the person really was and replacing them with some fictional character, nullifying their whole existence. Those from the old road are too honest for that. Our real-life characters mean too much to us.

I first started feeling under the weather in the late spring of the year I turned seventy. I was speaking in Galway and realised I felt short of breath. Following a string of doctor's visits, a solid month-long stay in Tallaght hospital and a near-death experience during my angiogram that was more of a non-experience, the doctors finally came back to me in the late summer with a diagnosis of fibrosis alveolitis, a progressive lung disease for which there is no cure and little treatment. I'm not used to being told to slow down but that's one of the phrases I hear most these days.

At the moment, I feel great. But I worry about what will happen to my pro-bono clients once I can't work and whether solicitors will take on their cases. I worry about the women's refuge and who will look after the women's cases there. I worry about what Evelyn will do without me. About missing out on more time with my children and grandchildren. That my favourite stories won't be told any longer. That the end will be miserable.

Both my parents' deaths were fast, unexpected, shocking. Especially in my father's case, there hadn't been enough time to settle things I'd have liked to settle; ask questions to which I'd have liked to know the answers. My mother's death was so difficult for me that even though I was in my forties when she passed away, I couldn't bear to be with her when it happened. She had been minding one of my sister's children in Howth and had a heart attack in the grocery store. I remember being in Bewley's with Margaret Gaj when one of the waitresses came over to tell me that Evelyn had rung looking for me to tell me the news. My mother survived the heart attack long enough to be taken to the hospital and she asked that I collect Mrs Davis and bring her up to visit. It was Mrs Davis who was in the room with her when she passed away. I know that a nurse asked her if she wanted a priest and she said no, that she had her family around her. It was just a few months before her eightieth birthday and she was living with us at the time. I know I would never have been ready to say goodbye to her, no matter what age she lived to.

My own death may be slower and more difficult than either of my parents' deaths. But even if there was a way to control these things, how is it possible to time a passing 'correctly'? How much time would be enough to say goodbye and in what way would I want to do it?

I have a few ideas. For starters, it helps that my family isn't at all shy about discussing the inevitable. They talk about my funeral in front of me and they plan to play the Johnny Cash song, 'Ring of Fire'. I think that's perfect with its theme of the all-consuming nature of (in Cash's and his wife June Carter's case, forbidden) love. Cash claimed that the famous, bright opening trumpet melody came to him in a dream. It's a song that suits a life-long, hopeless romantic. It also has the added twist that those not paying close attention to the lyrics could easily assume the song is about hell, especially at the chorus: 'I fell into a burning ring of fire.//I fell down, down, down and the flames went higher.// And it burns, burns, burns, the ring of fire...'

One summer's day shortly before my seventieth birthday, when I was newly home after my month in the hospital, Evelyn brought a suit jacket she'd bought for me into the sitting room where I was talking to one of my daughters. She asked me to try it on. 'I didn't want to buy it for you while you were still in the hospital, in case you died,' she deadpanned. 'Waste of money.' I put it on and walked around, unconvinced. My daughter cleared up any doubts. 'You look fat,' she said matter-of-factly. 'You can barely button it.' So that was that.

I do like the idea of having a funeral before I actually die so I can hear what everyone has to say about me but that's basically what my sixtieth birthday party was. It was shortly after my heart bypass surgery and I hadn't fully expected to see sixty, so I figured it was a just cause for celebration. Now, more than ten years later, I'm suspicious that Evelyn will be tempted to have a funeral Mass of some sort for me in the church. She's already told me that I'll never know what happens; I'll be dead and what should I care? When I think about my real feelings about death, one of Woody Allen's classic quips comes to mind: 'I'm not afraid of dying, I'd just rather not be there when it happens.' I made peace long ago with the reality of death and the naturalness of life cycles. If I could just skip the dying part, I'd be fine.

In October 2006, I was invited to NUI Galway to be on the panel of a debate about euthanasia and ended up not being able to make it because of a bad chest infection. I was chuffed when they postponed the whole debate for me. I think the issues around euthanasia are some of the most important that need to be sorted out now for the next generation. They said we'd never see legal contraception in Ireland. Then they said we'd never see divorce. They say we'll never see abortion and they're wrong about that. It's inevitable. Just as it's inevitable that we'll see controlled voluntary euthanasia too.

I know I won't live to see legalised euthanasia in Ireland and maybe my children won't either but I think it's possible my grandchildren will. I have a vision of how it will work. Everyone will be allowed to live to a respectable old age, say eighty-five. Then right after reaching the designated age, they will be contacted individually with a warm message saying something along the lines of, 'Congratulations! You've been invited to the room of forgetfulness, where we will celebrate your life and give you a nice send-off.'

I joke. But I know there are a lot worse ways to go. I also know, as sure as night follows day, that we will have gay marriages. I will probably not be alive to celebrate but I'm happy to know that these changes will come about.

One morning during my month in the hospital, I got a call on my mobile (which, to borrow a phrase from Charlton Heston about his gun, would have to be pried out of my cold, dead hands before I'd give it up) from a researcher on the popular RTÉ morning radio programme, *The Tubridy Show*. They invited me to come on to the show to talk about my recent 'Unsung Hero of Dublin' award from the Dublin City Council. The Women's Refuge in Rathmines had nominated me for my twenty-odd years of service there. Once the nurses in the hospital found out what I did for a living, my room turned into a kind of legal-aid clinic for the staff. I couldn't have been happier as hospital stays of any length get very boring.

I had to get permission from the doctors and arrange for transportation from Tallaght to RTÉ's studio in Donnybrook. One of the things I wanted to make sure I said on the air was that in my twenty years of providing legal services to the women in the refuge, there was never a time when I couldn't find some junior or senior counsel somewhere to work on a case with me for free. I think that's very important to mention, when so many people look on barristers as mercenary bastards.

The whole affair exhausted me for days afterwards but going on the show had two immediate advantages and a third I knew nothing about until later: firstly, it got me out of the hospital room I'd been stuck in for weeks and secondly, it was an interview, which I never shy away from and usually enjoy immensely.

The third walked into my room that night – a woman I didn't

recognise at first, bearing a big bouquet of flowers.

'I don't expect you to recognise me,' she said. 'But I heard you on the radio this morning and I remember you.' Thirteen years earlier, she had been outside the family law court at Dolphin House, utterly distraught, at the beginning of the proceedings for her case. I was finishing up a case I'd worked on inside and was leaving when I saw her. I went over to her and instead of asking, 'Are you all right?' to which the answer was clear, I said, 'Are you legally represented?'

'I can't afford it,' she said miserably.

'Would you like me to represent you?' I asked.

'I just told you, I can't afford it,' she said.

'I didn't say anything about money. I just asked if you wanted me to represent you,' I said. My barrister argued her case for her and we got a great result.

'I just wanted you to know I never forgot it,' she said to me in my hospital room.

At my seventieth birthday party a few years ago at St Jude's GAA club, we passed around After Eight dinner mints in boxes in those delicate, slim, dark-drown wrappers. When the guests pulled out the contents of the wrappers, they got a surprise. Instead of the mints, someone in my family had figured out that the dimensions of the wrappers were perfect for holding condoms and that's what we gave out for favours. We picked the Durex Extra-Safe variety and put home-made stickers on the packaging showing a smiling condom with the title 'Crummey Condoms' on one side and the inscription 'Going Strong for 70 Years' on the reverse. Some of my grandchildren were circulating around the tables with real boxes of mints, to keep people guessing whether they'd pick a chocolate or a condom.

Sometimes I have to remind myself how extraordinary it is that Irish people in their twenties don't know what it's like not to be able to get condoms in a shop, or even to have to ask a chemist to get them from behind the counter. The results of all those protests, meetings, newspaper articles and television debates fade as time goes on, a generation begins to die and the changes we fought so hard for morph into what we always hoped they'd become – the status quo. Those changes that sparked so much fury in the beginning are invisible but profound.

Occasionally we're reminded of the worst of our past and, unlike the best of our progress, it can't be permitted to fade away into the backdrop of daily life without collective introspection. The release in May 2009 of the Ryan Report on the abuse of Irish children in state-run institutions shocked the nation and spurred weeks of outrage, solidarity marches and a revisiting of painful memories for thousands of victims. The report, which was conducted by the Commission to Inquire into Child Abuse, took nearly ten years to compile and gathered evidence from as far back as 1914 but focused mainly on the period from the 1930s to the 1970s. It is nearly 3000 pages long, with the first-hand testimony of 1700 men and women of abuse they suffered in various institutions. More than half of them reported being sexually abused. Eighteen religious orders and 216 institutions were named in victims' testimony. More than eight hundred individual priests, nuns, Christian Brothers and lay people were identified as carrying out the crimes but these names were not released to the public. This caused public uproar and questions as to why our government felt it needed to shield the perpetrators from scrutiny or prosecution. For many, it felt as if like the abusers got away with it.

The report includes eight full chapters on the Christian Brothers. They ran the largest number of institutions for boys in the country and were the subject of more allegations than all the other male orders combined. The letters pages of *The Irish Times* were flooded with people expressing sympathy for the victims, rage at the perpetrators, the Church and the Department of Education for condoning and ignoring the abuse and also letters from some victims themselves. Then there was the issue of compensation, which the government had previously capped at €128 million in total contributions from the eighteen orders combined. As of the end of May 2009, the Residential Institutions Redress Board (a separate body from the Ryan Commission set up to process claim applications) had received approximately 15,000 applications and estimated that the total cost of awards would top €1 billion.

While stories of horrific child abuse at the hands of Church members have been emerging for at least the last decade, the anger over the Ryan Report was a groundswell of emotion the likes of which I haven't seen in a long time. The report revealed, finally, that the cases of abuse we'd heard about were not anomalies. They were not the result of a few 'bad apples' in the orders. They were not the exceptions. They were the norm. I think it was only when the evidence surfaced that they weren't isolated incidents and that it was systemic abuse perpetuated over decades and across orders that most people could fully comprehend the extent of the damage that was done to our children.

I wrote my own letter to *The Irish Times*, which was published in the end of May 2009. In it, I outlined my work with Reform, the first, famous case we had taken against the Christian Brothers and the events around the first *Late Late Show* devoted to the subject of abuse in the schools. I also said I wanted to draw a distinction I thought extremely important between Irish priests and the Irish Christian Brothers. There may have been good priests who were unaware that some of their colleagues were abusing our children but in my opinion there were two categories of Christian Brothers: those who brutalised our children and those who stood idly by. Ever since I was a student in Crumlin CBS, that's how I've felt and the report's findings served to reinforce my opinion.

I also wrote about how the publication of the Ryan report caused me a lot of upset, that I couldn't sleep the night the report came out and that I couldn't help but wonder if I had tried hard enough all these years. I finished my letter: 'I would now suggest that the Irish Christian Brothers show some humility and stop trying to obstruct justice and instead donate their wealth to a children's charitable organisation, keeping just enough to feed their elderly brothers. They should then fold their tents and fade quietly into the night.' To me, the Christian Brothers should be a proscribed organisation, on the basis that they committed as many atrocities as the IRA ever did.

I received some letters myself in the following weeks that gave me a bit of a lift. One thing that struck me about the letters was that a good few of them were from outside Ireland, which indicated how closely people all over the world were paying attention to the report's findings. People in America, Helsinki, Brussels and different parts of Ireland wrote to me to share their thoughts. One from an Irish man in Brussels read simply, 'I share the shame and guilt of a whole nation. If only there had been more like you.' Others wrote to talk about their own memories of abuse and still others to say they were happy that I had lived long enough to be vindicated. Of course, I'm pleased that the full extent of institutional abuse has finally been exposed and proven, because I feel that it's a small step toward justice. But on the issue of 'vindication' I have to say that I would rather have been able to make more progress at the time – and to have done it more quickly – than to experience that vindication at this point in my life.

The publication of the Murphy report in November 2009 further proved not only how widespread the abuse was but how the Gardai had colluded with the Church in covering it up for decades. The Murphy report focused on Dublin and confirmed that four former Dublin archbishops – John Charles McQuaid, Dermot Ryan, Kevin McNamara and Cardinal Desmond Connell – had known about the abuse but had done nothing to stop it. Cardinal Connell has retired and the other three are deceased;

there were also forty-six priests named as abusers in the report, eleven of whom have pleaded guilty to sexual assault or have been convicted. The rest are either dead or have eluded punishment. The report details some shocking admissions of guilt. One priest admitted to abusing more than a hundred children, while another said he committed an act of abuse about once every two weeks consistently over a period of twenty-five years. For me, the conclusions of both reports demonstrated what I had always known was as much a tragedy as the abuse itself: a whole nation's ability to stand silently by and let it happen.

I think it's a good idea for me to keep trying things I haven't done before, especially at my age. Very recently, a lady I know who lives in Massachusetts and was getting married in Ireland asked me if I would officiate at her ceremony. I was delighted, so I sent away to the Massachusetts Governor, Deval Patrick, for all the papers I needed and got my certification. I'm chuffed that I qualified to perform the marriage and I love weddings. In a way, it makes me a little like a priest, which I'm sure is a terrifying thought for some.

I've got my family, friends, work and stories and I'm pleased to think the stories will endure. I still think one of the loveliest phrases in the English language is, 'Let's go for lunch.' And I still love driving around Dublin city and delighting in it as it reminds me of some of those stories, especially if there's someone new in the passenger seat to tell them to.